D0502312

# The Wit & Wisdom of Harry Truman

*Books of similar interest from Random House Value Publishing:*

THE WIT & WISDOM OF OSCAR WILDE

THE WIT & WISDOM OF ABRAHAM LINCOLN

THE ESSENTIAL ABRAHAM LINCOLN

THE ESSENTIAL FRANKLIN DELANO ROOSEVELT

THE ESSENTIAL THEODORE ROOSEVELT

# The Wit & Wisdom of Harry Truman

## A Treasury of Quotations, Anecdotes, and Observations

Ralph Keyes

Gramercy Books
New York

This 1999 edition is published by Gramercy Books™, an imprint of Random House Value Publishing, Inc. 201 East 50th Street, New York, N.Y. 10022, by arrangement with the Doe Coover Agency, Winchester, Mass.

Gramercy Books™ and colophon are trademarks of Random House Value Publishing, Inc.

Random House
New York • Toronto • London • Sydney • Auckland
http://www.randomhouse.com/

Printed and bound in the United States of America.

**Library of Congress Cataloging-in-Publication Data**

Truman, Harry S., 1884-1972.
The wit & wisdom of Harry Truman : a treasury of quotations anecdotes, and observations / [edited by] Ralph Keyes.
p. cm.
Originally published: New York : HarperCollins, 1995.
Includes bibliographical references and index.
ISBN 0-517-19459-7
1. Truman, Harry S., 1884-1972 Quotations. 2. United States—Politics and government—1945-1989 Quotations, maxims, etc. 3. Quotations, American. I. Keyes, Ralph II. Title. III. Title: Wit and wisdom of Harry Truman.
[E472.5.T62 1999]
973.918'092—dc21 99-14883
CIP

8 7 6 5 4 3 2 1

*For my brother Gene,*
*who has always given me a hand*

# *Contents*

# Acknowledgments

I would like to acknowledge help from the following people in writing this book: Layne Longfellow and Walter Rhodes for general encouragement and manuscript review; the staffs of the Yellow Springs and Antioch College libraries—Jan Miller especially—for invaluable research assistance; and Robert Ferrell for consultation on sources.

My agent, Colleen Mohyde, and editor, Hugh Van Dusen, gave me good support throughout this project. My sons, David and Scott, pitched in by helping to do photocopying. As ever, my wife, Muriel, gave me the most help of all: with research, manuscript criticism, and creating time for me to spend on this manuscript. Thanks, Muriel.

# *Author's Note*

As is customary in compilations of this kind, I've occasionally made small alterations of Harry Truman's words for the sake of consistency and clarity. At times this has been done to correct spelling or grammar (not Truman's strong suits). On occasion it meant trimming throat-clearing words or phrases ("one might say," "in my opinion," etc.). Editing within quotations is indicated by ellipses. For the sake of visual grace I have capitalized words at the beginning of remarks whose actual beginning has been pruned, and put periods at the end of comments with edited endings. An occasional paragraph has been broken up. Others have been run together. This has all been done for reading ease, and to best convey Harry Truman's thoughts. While making such minor changes of form, I have bent over backward to remain true to his *meaning*. Any words added to clarify a remark are placed in brackets. Not one word of Truman's has been changed in this compilation. To the contrary, by using original sources whenever possible, I've sometimes been able to restore his actual words when others took the liberty of rewriting them.

# The Wit & Wisdom of Harry Truman

# *Wilder Than Ever About Harry*

> *I am ready to hazard an opinion, to which I came, I confess manfully, with dragging feet, that Harry S. Truman will eventually win a place as President alongside Jefferson and Theodore Roosevelt. . . . He was fascinating to watch, even when the sight hurt, and he will be fascinating to read about.*
>
> —CLINTON ROSSITER
> *The American Presidency*

In an era of spin doctors, media consultants, and government by poll, it's refreshing to read the words of a man who knew his mind and wasn't afraid to speak it.

That man was Harry Truman. The plainspoken man from Missouri is enjoying a renaissance. In his lifetime, it was said with a snicker that Harry Truman proved *anyone* could be president. Now that's said with pride. Since Truman's death in 1972, Democrats and

Republicans alike have praised him as a model citizen-president. Gerald Ford kept a bust of Truman in the Oval Office. Ronald Reagan caught Truman's words but missed the melody with his Steuben glass plaque engraved THE BUCK STOPS HERE. George Bush even ran in 1992 as a "Truman Republican." (One can only imagine what Harry himself would have said about that oxymoron.)

The glow surrounding Truman as an ex-president stands in stark contrast to his dim reputation while in office. During seven and a half years in the White House, Truman seemed hokey to many. Parochial. A president who couldn't wait to leave Washington for Independence, Missouri. One who wore loud shirts, called his wife "The Boss," and liked to show off his so-so piano playing. Harry Truman looked more like a Rotary club president than a U.S. president. He stood for a front porch, double-breasted way of life many postwar Americans were trying to flee. Jet-setters like Jack and Jacqueline appealed to us more than ice cream socialites such as Harry and Bess.

Today we feel differently. Now we're hungry for Harry Truman's type of American. In the age of Prozac, we admire his lack of angst. In a time of skepticism, we're nostalgic for Truman's optimism. His rigid sense of duty compares favorably with our flexible hedonism. During an era of dysfunctional families—including those of presidents—we enjoy reading about his close one. There's something irresistible about a powerful world leader in his sixties who considered his wife "my sweetheart."

Unlike his eloquent predecessor, Truman didn't use what he called "$40 words." Quite the contrary. Truman's comments were filled with terms such as "hooey," "high hat," and "nincompoop." He didn't pussyfoot around. Truman seldom left any doubt about his positions. "I never sit on a fence," he said. "I am either on one side or another."

Unlike his successor—whose strategy for dealing with reporters was to "confuse 'em"—evasion was not Harry Truman's style. He never had to struggle to make things "perfectly clear." There was no talk of a credibility gap during Truman's administration. It's hard to imagine anyone calling him "Slick Harry."

Truman's candor had him in hot water for much of his presidency. His colorful language made many a listener wince. Only after he returned to Missouri were we able to step back and wonder what could have bothered us so much about this outspoken man. "The quirks and quips that gave the press a field day throughout his presidency seem less defects now than a refreshing naturalness," observed biographer Robert H. Ferrell.

Harry Truman stands in stark contrast to modern politicians who don't seem sure of what they stand for until they've taken a poll. This doesn't mean that his successors have been liars or four-flushers (although Nixon was). Rather, post-Truman politicians as a group seem to have little sense of self, of character, of values other than the value of getting elected. Contemporaries observed repeatedly that Harry Truman *knew who he was.* "I've never met anyone," wrote journalist Charles Robbins, "whose idea of his own identity was clearer than Truman's."

At the heart of this identity was Truman's conviction that he was one of us. Franklin Delano Roosevelt befriended the common man. Harry S. Truman was the common man in person. Truman wasn't *for* the people so much as he was *of* the people. We saw him as a peer. That's the way he saw himself. "I look just like any other fifty people you meet in the street," Truman once observed.

America is still filled with people who exchanged a word or two with President Truman. One World War II veteran recalled passing him while out for an early morning stroll. "Hi, soldier," said Truman to the man in uniform. "Hi, Harry," responded the serviceman. Imagine calling Franklin Roosevelt "Frank." Yet Americans routinely called Truman by his nickname. How did he feel about this? "All over the country they call me 'Harry,'" he said. "I like it. I believe when you speak to me like that you like me."

While driving a cab as a student in New York, Mike Gravel pulled up beside the strolling former president. "Young man," said Truman, sticking his hand through the cab window, "you look good to me. Just make something of yourself." After Gravel was elected to the U.S. Senate from Alaska, they met again. What struck the new senator was how little difference there was in his two encounters with Truman. "A cab driver and a U.S. Senator got the same attention and respect from him," said Gravel.

One reason we recall Truman so fondly is that it's not hard to put ourselves in his size-9 shoes. Who among us hasn't fantasized about waking up one morning to find ourselves president? Truman not only lived that fantasy, but proved to be up to the job. His example suggests that we all have untapped resources of strength, decisiveness, and ability to grow.

Truman didn't covet the presidency. Quite the contrary. Throughout his time in office he spoke constantly of his wish to flee the "Great White Jail." When Press Secretary Charles Ross observed that he'd rather be right than president, Truman said that he'd rather be *anything* than president. But *duty* was Harry Truman's cardinal virtue. Truman genuinely thought he had work to do for his country whether or not he felt like doing it. One reason we admire

Truman so much in retrospect was the stand-up way he shouldered a crushing burden that he hadn't sought, didn't want, and couldn't wait to pass along. So why did he run for reelection in 1948? Although a genuinely reluctant president, Truman was also a proud man who couldn't abide the thought that he was keeping Franklin Roosevelt's seat warm while Americans chose his *real* successor. Truman wanted that title for himself, and earned it.

Even after being elected in his own right, Harry Truman never forgot that he was president due to circumstances beyond his control. Perhaps that's why he was better able than most presidents to stay human beneath the twenty-one-gun salutes. Truman always kept in mind that he was a tenant in the White House, not its owner. One almost had a sense that he saw himself as an actor playing the part of a world leader, and doing so superbly. "As Harry Truman, I'm not very much," he said, "but as President Truman I have no peer."

Truman's ability to grow into the presidency was his greatest asset. This meant that he had to transcend a parochial background and some backwater prejudices. The man from Missouri could be surprisingly petty: right on the big issues, wrong on the small ones, said House Speaker Sam Rayburn. The president who recognized Israel minutes after its founding had mocked Jews in letters to Bess. The man who did more for civil rights than any president since Lincoln sprinkled his conversation with racial epithets. The decisiveness we admire so much in Harry Truman could be seen as rushing to judgment. Many historians have questioned the long-term consequences of his decisions, such as those to develop the hydrogen bomb, found the Central Intelligence Agency, and expand the presidency into today's imperial version. Posing such questions about

Truman doesn't mean that we can't admire him nonetheless. "I am not sure he was right about the atomic bomb, or even Korea," Eric Sevareid told David McCullough. "But remembering him reminds people what a man in that office ought to be like. It's character, just character. He stands like a rock in memory now."

That helps explain why we're wilder than ever about Harry. We can't seem to quench our thirst for information about this fascinating man. Several excellent biographies have been written about Truman, most recently by David McCullough and Robert H. Ferrell. Ferrell has done yeoman work editing and publishing Truman's letters, diaries, and miscellaneous writing. So have Monte Poen, and Margaret Truman, who has also written biographies of her father and mother. She and David Gallen have based separate books on a series of taped reflections by Truman (*Where the Buck Stops* and *The Quotable Harry S. Truman*). Truman himself published his memoirs and a follow-up work called *Mister Citizen.*

What we don't have is a book that distills the best of Harry Truman's words into one accessible volume. Thus *The Wit & Wisdom of Harry Truman.* This book combines the most cogent remarks by Truman with fuller observations from his diary, letters, and speeches. Excerpts from Truman's press conferences show his gift for peppery repartee. Anecdotes that illustrate different facets of his character—"Harry Truman's Life Stories"—give a more rounded picture of the man.

For a compiler of Trumaniana, the problem is not what to include but what to leave out. Truman made enough wise, witty observations to fill this volume and many more. Even his public papers serve up nuggets of humor and verve. In the give-'em-hell speeches of 1948, Truman's words bristle off the page. "This Republican

Congress has already stuck a pitchfork in the farmer's back," he told an Iowa audience. "I wish I could stay longer," Truman said in Illinois, "but I have to get back to Washington to veto some more bills." From the back of his train car he warned yet a third crowd, "If you send another Republican Congress to Washington, you're a bigger bunch of suckers than I think you are!"

Because he was so outspoken, it's tempting to include only Truman's saltier remarks in a book such as this. But there was more to Harry Truman than salt and pepper. For a man of action, he was unusually reflective. Truman may not have been brilliant. Nor was he well educated in the conventional sense. But—like so many whose love of books hasn't been extinguished by four years of college—Truman read voraciously; history and biography especially. If his intellect wasn't profound, it was intelligent and wide-ranging. Truman made continual thoughtful observations about the issues of his day. Many of these observations bear on issues of our own day: congressional term limits, for example, the federal deficit, and national health insurance. Some are strikingly prescient. *The Wit & Wisdom of Harry Truman* includes a fair measure of his more thoughtful comments to balance the many "Trumanisms," with particular emphasis on topics such as leadership, decision making, and the presidency, where he spoke from experience.

*The Wit & Wisdom of Harry Truman* can be used in two ways:

1. As a mini-biography to be read straight through
2. As a browser and resource

One is tempted to add a third category: as a primer of clear, vigorous exposition. It's a pleasant surprise to discover how vivid a writer Truman could be. After he and Bess enjoyed a summer supper on the south porch of the White House, for example, Truman jotted this vignette:

> *A robin hops around looking for worms, finds one and pulls with all his might to unearth him. A mocking bird imitates robins, jays, red birds, crows, hawks—but has no individual note of his own. A lot of people like that. Planes take off and land at the National Air Port south of the Jefferson Memorial. It is a lovely evening. I can see the old Chesapeake and Potomac Canal going across the Washington Monument grounds, barges anchoring west of the Monument. I can see old J. Q. Adams going swimming in it and getting his clothes stolen by an angry woman who wanted a job. The old guy did not have my guards or it wouldn't have happened. Then I wake up, go upstairs and go to work and contemplate the prison life of a president. What the hell!*

Harry Truman was a spirited man. This book tries to capture his spirit. That means not just the rip-roaring campaigner of 1948 but the compassionate man revered by his colleagues. It's no accident that Harry Truman was never the subject of an unflattering memoir by an associate. Yet he was paid many a tribute by those with whom he worked. The more we learn about Truman's persona, the better he looks. If anything—unlike the case with so many of history's "greats"—what we've discovered about Truman's private life only adds to his luster.

Although the last of nineteenth-century men in his sensibilities, Truman's spirit was in tune with our times—or, should we say, the times we'd like to have. "In a way," said Michigan Senator Philip Hart in his eulogy to Truman, "I suppose, it could be argued that he did the public a disservice by teaching the people that candor and politics, honesty and government are not incompatible items. After President Truman, the public—not unreasonably—expected complete straightforwardness and frankness from everybody elected to Federal office thereafter. The disappointment was inevitable.

"He was a great man, yes, but he has given us a gift that we do not always get from great men—he gave us the gift of warm, smiling memories."

*The Wit & Wisdom of Harry Truman* is an attempt to capture that warmth, and convey those smiles along with the thoughtful insights of a dedicated public man.

# *Truman on People*

WINSTON CHURCHILL

✍ He is a most charming and a very clever person—meaning clever in the English, not the Kentucky sense.

✍ He gave me a lot of hooey about how great my country is and how he loved Roosevelt and how he intended to love me etc., etc.

✍ He was as windy as old Langer [North Dakota Senator William Langer], but he knew his English language and after he'd talked half an hour there'd be at least one gem of a sentence and two thoughts maybe which could have been expressed in four minutes.

✍ The greatest public figure of our time.

DOUGLAS MACARTHUR

✍ Our great bald-headed general, with the dyed hair.

✍ Mr. Prima Donna, Brass Hat, Five Star MacArthur. He's worse than the Cabots and the Lodges—at least they talked with one another before they told God what to do. Mac tells God right off.

GEORGE MARSHALL

❧ General Marshall is one of the most astute and profound men I have ever known.

❧ The more I see and talk to him, the more certain I am he's the great one of the age.

## MISCELLANEOUS

BERNARD BARUCH

❧ He wants to run the world, the moon and maybe Jupiter.

JOHN BROWN

❧ A fanatic, a murderer, and a troublemaker. One of the best things Robert E. Lee ever did was to hang old John Brown.

WILLIAM JENNINGS BRYAN

❧ One of the most misunderstood and underestimated men in American history.

GEORGE CUSTER

❧ The Douglas MacArthur of his day.

CHARLES DE GAULLE

❧ A pinhead.

WILLIAM FULBRIGHT

An overeducated s.o.b.

BARRY GOLDWATER

A damn fool.

JOSEPH KENNEDY

As big a crook as we've got anywhere in this country.

JOSEPH McCARTHY

A pathological liar.

VYACHESLAV MOLOTOV

A perfect mutton head.

PABLO PICASSO

A French Communist caricaturist.

WILL ROGERS

Almost a second Mark Twain. . . . I'm glad his mother didn't believe in birth control.

JOSEPH STALIN

He was anything but insane . . . he was a smart hombre.

MARK TWAIN

A kind of charlatan and fakir—but all natives of Missouri love him.

DANIEL WEBSTER

A windbag. He made a great many orations, and I imagine he did a very good job, but he was still a windbag.

WALTER WINCHELL

If Winchell ever told the truth it was by accident and not intentional.

## PRESIDENTS

GEORGE WASHINGTON

Washington was as tough as a bird could be and he used language that the artilleryman understands when he got wrought.

He was a pompous man in some ways. When he went to state affairs, for example, he wore velvet and satin and diamond knee-buckles and powdered his hair.

When the decisions were hard to make, he made them, and he carried them through.

JOHN ADAMS

He still had in the back of his head that there ought to be a ruling class in the country.

I'm sure Adams never really got over the fact that Jefferson had clearly been a better president than he'd been.

THOMAS JEFFERSON

❧ The Adamses and the New England historians made a crook and atheist out of Thomas Jefferson until honest research proved 'em in error (to put it mildly).

❧ He was one of the brainiest men of his time.

❧ He was a master politician, and this helped make him a great leader.

JAMES MADISON

❧ When he became president, he was like every other man of considerable brain power and education: He found it difficult to make decisions.

JOHN QUINCY ADAMS

❧ The single really interesting thing about Adams, I'm afraid, is that he was the only son of a president in our history to become president himself.

ANDREW JACKSON

❧ One thing I always liked about Jackson was that he brought the basic issues into clear focus. People knew what he stood for and what he was against.

❧ He represented the man with a hole in his pocket just as much as he represented the big shots.

❧ I have no wish to prettify him. He doesn't need it. He was stubborn. He was tactless. Often he was ungracious to the point of being surly.

MARTIN VAN BUREN

Van Buren was a schemer. He was a maneuverer, as you can see in all organizations.

I've got to say that our country would have done just as well not to have had Van Buren as president.

JOHN TYLER

He was a contrary old son of a bitch.

JAMES POLK

Polk was a man who knew what he wanted to do and did it. He was an executive like we dream about, and very seldom see.

Upon his retirement he said, "I now retire as a servant and regain my position as a sovereign." He was absolutely right. I have been through it and I know.

ZACHARY TAYLOR

I can't be charitable and say that he failed to carry out his program; he didn't have any program to carry out.

FRANKLIN PIERCE

Though he looked the way people who make movies think a president should look, he didn't pay any more attention to business as president of the United States than the man in the moon, and he really made a mess of things.

Pierce was a nincompoop.

ABRAHAM LINCOLN

❧ One of the things that so endears him to everybody is the fact that he was just a common everyday citizen, was glad to admit it and act like one.

❧ Lincoln was just himself, and that's the sort of man I admire.

❧ Lincoln *had* to make decisions and take chances, and he studied each situation and made decisions that he felt were best for the people of the United States and for the rest of the world, and that's the reason he turned out to be a great president.

❧ If Lincoln had lived, he would have done no better than Johnson.

ANDREW JOHNSON

❧ Johnson did his level best to be a constitutional president, and he knew more about the Constitution than any man ever in the White House.

❧ He had plenty of nerve and he knew what he wanted to do and he was willing to make decisions.

❧ I guess next to George Washington, the most tolerant and enlightened man in the White House.

ULYSSES S. GRANT

❧ The worst president in our history.

❧ Grant was typical of the soldier-president. Without any

understanding of political machinery, he was able to ride into office on the popularity which military victory always brings.

He wasn't even a chief executive; he was another sleepwalker whose administration was even more crooked than Warren Harding's, if that's possible.

GROVER CLEVELAND

Cleveland was a good president because he was familiar with the powers of an executive, and unlike some of his predecessors, he wasn't afraid to use them.

BENJAMIN HARRISON

I tend to pair up Benjamin Harrison and Dwight Eisenhower because they're the two presidents I can think of who most preferred laziness to labor.

THEODORE ROOSEVELT

A little man in a long Prince Albert coat to make him look taller.

Teddy Roosevelt was often more bull, without the moose, than substance.

Teddy . . . made a great publicity stunt out of being a trust-buster, but in fact he busted very few of them.

WILLIAM HOWARD TAFT

A fat, jolly, likable, mediocre man.

WOODROW WILSON

Woodrow Wilson served as a constant example to me of how to operate and function as president of the United States.

He wanted almost desperately to help people and improve the world around him, but he was no bundle of laughs.

Wilson had the idea that he was *the* smartest man in the United States . . . of course people associated with him didn't like that attitude, but it's probably the truth.

Woodrow Wilson was the first one who realized the world position of the United States. Wilson tried to make a world power out of us. He was far ahead of his time. In fact, he was thirty-one years ahead of his time in his League of Nations proposal.

WARREN HARDING

Alice Roosevelt Longworth . . . once said about him, "Harding was not a bad man. He was just a slob." I think she was being entirely too kind.

CALVIN COOLIDGE

The man who got more rest than any previous president.

HERBERT HOOVER

In a political way, [he] started at the top instead of at the bottom and it would be just like my starting into his engineering career without knowing anything about engineering.

I hold him in high esteem as a man of character and capacity and talent, and he deserved better treatment at the hands of his own party.

FRANKLIN ROOSEVELT

He was a great executive, but he was not a good administrator.

I think Franklin Roosevelt did the very best he could under the circumstances, and the only thing I am sorry about is that his health failed and he didn't live until the end of his fourth term.

I always thought Franklin Roosevelt came nearer being the ideal president than anyone we'd had during my lifetime.

DWIGHT EISENHOWER

A decent man, but a bad president.

The General doesn't know any more about politics than a pig knows about Sunday.

He is not as intelligent as I thought. Evidently his staff has furnished the intelligence.

Nonaction was characteristic of Eisenhower as president because he proved to be such a dumb son of a bitch when he got out of his uniform.

It's interesting that a single thing, that great smile of Eisenhower's, gave him the worldwide and lifelong reputation of being a sunny and amiable man, when those of us who knew him well were all too well aware that he was essentially a surly, angry, and disagreeable man.

❧ Eisenhower looked out of the window or played golf or read one of those Westerns by Luke Short he was always reading when he should have been taking decisive action.

❧ Eisenhower really didn't *do* anything or *decide* anything. He passed the buck, down.

JOHN F. KENNEDY

❧ It's not the Pope who worries me, it's the Pop.

❧ I felt he was too immature.

❧ I am sure that all of you know that before the Democratic convention made its choice, I was supporting another candidate. At the convention, Jack Kennedy won the nomination. I'm from Missouri, you know, and I have to be shown. Well, Kennedy showed me.

❧ I think that young fella might just make a hell of a fine president.

RICHARD NIXON

❧ Mr. Nixon lacks the moral sensitivity which the occupant of the White House should possess . . . he is impetuous, quick to act, rash, and on occasions his conduct is irresponsible.

❧ He is a dangerous man. Never has there been one like him so close to the presidency.

❧ A mean, nasty fellow.

❧ I don't like Nixon and I never will.

# *Truman on Issues*

AMERICANS

ɞ If you want to talk about one hundred percent Americans, you must go back to the inhabitants of the United States at the time that Europeans first landed.

ɞ The acts of stupidity through the ages did us a kind of unintentional favor—by driving so many different kinds of good people to our shores and merging them together as Americans.

ɞ The United States was created by the boys and girls who could not get along at home.

BELIEFS

ɞ I've never really believed in capital punishment. I commuted the sentence of the fellow who was trying to shoot me to life imprisonment. That's the best example I can give you.

ɞ There is nothing in the world I dislike more than a stuffed shirt. Stick a pin in the shirt and the wind comes out, and then you will find out that he is a counterfeit.

ꕥ My own sympathy has always been with the little fellow, the man without advantages.

ꕥ I was never for the underdog, in turn, becoming the top dog with complete power to act. When the underdog gets power, he too often turns out to be an even more brutal top dog.

ꕥ I am sorry to see a growth of snobbery in the United States in recent years. I especially deplore the tendency to look down on people who work with their hands.

ꕥ We need men with great intellects, need their ideas. But we need to balance them with other kinds of people too.

ꕥ I am not in favor of erecting memorials to people who are living. I think it is bad business because a person may do something before he dies that will make the people want to tear the memorial down.

ꕥ Good name and honor are worth more than all the gold and jewels ever mined.

## CAMPAIGNING

ꕥ Cut your speech to twenty-five minutes, shake hands with as many people as you can for a little while. Afterward, even if you have time left, leave. If you have no place to go, you can always pull off the road and take a nap.

ꕥ Don't attack your opponent. Whenever you do, it only gives him free advertising and another chance to attack you. Let him attack you if he will, but you will be all right if you stick to the issues.

❧ I always put myself in the place of the voter when I am thinking of his reaction.

❧ I do not approve of "front porch" campaigns. I never liked to see any man elected to office who did not go out and meet the people in person and work for their votes.

❧ You have to get around and listen to what people are saying. Dewey learned that in '48. He didn't listen, he just talked—and didn't say much, either.

❧ When a candidate for the presidency stands in front of the people, the people get a chance to analyze his character in a way they can't from television and radio.

❧ A man is never quite himself on a television program. He can only be himself when he personally meets people face to face. Only then can the people fully understand what a man stands for. In personal appearance, he has to be just himself without the benefit of makeup.

❧ If a politician is on your side and he gets headlines, that is favorable advertising; if he is on the other side and gets headlines that are not in your corner, he is a publicity hound.

❧ I'm not so sure that people have the respect for the big money that everybody thinks they have, because they like to vote for a poor man sometimes.

ℰ𝒮 You know my program was "Give 'em Hell" and if they don't like it, give 'em more hell.

ℰ𝒮 I never did give anybody hell. I just told the truth and they thought it was hell.

ℰ𝒮 I always feel a sympathy for a defeated candidate and for his supporters and workers. No matter how wrong he may be on principle or record he is badly hurt by defeat. I know because I've been through it.

ℰ𝒮 I have been skinned many a time on things by political opponents. But I never carried over any grudges . . . When campaigns are over and the people have made their decision, I believe personal feuds ought to end there.

ℰ𝒮 Every political battle I have I fight with everything I've got, and when it's over I get hold of my opponent and we have a bourbon and branch and say, "What can we do for the country?"

## CHILDREN

ℰ𝒮 I have found the best way to give advice to your children is to find out what they want and then advise them to do it.

ℰ𝒮 Advice to grandchildren is usually wasted. If the second and third generations *could* profit by the experience of the first generation, we would not be having some of the troubles we have today.

ℰ𝒮 Children nowadays have too many gadgets to fool with and not enough chores.

❦ Mama and Papa are more to blame [for delinquency] than the kids; parents should stay home and raise their children and spend less time in taverns.

❦ You can still do something with high school youths, but the college kids are different. They think they know everything.

❦ I always tell students that it is what you learn after you know it all that counts.

CIVIL LIBERTY

❦ Everyone has the right to express what he thinks. That, of course, lets the crackpots in. But if you cannot tell a crackpot when you see one, you ought to be taken in.

❦ You cannot stop the spread of an idea by passing a law against it. You cannot stamp out communism by driving it underground. You can prevent communism by more and better democracy.

❦ There were no communists in the State Department. That was a bunch of hooey and it never was proved. McCarthy started out with 105, and then got down to 80, then down to 30, then down to 12, and then didn't find any.

❦ I think the House Un-American Activities Committee . . . was the most un-American thing in America.

❦ There is no more fundamental axiom of American freedom than the familiar statement: In a free country, we punish men for the crimes they commit, but never for the opinions they have.

## CIVIL RIGHTS

❧ Religious and racial persecution is moronic at all times, perhaps the most idiotic of human stupidities.

❧ Whether discrimination is based on race, or creed, or color, or land of origin, it is utterly contrary to American ideals of democracy.

❧ When I was president, many people advised me not to raise the whole question of civil rights. They said it would make things worse. But you can't cure a moral problem by ignoring it. It is no service to the country to turn away from the hard problems—to ignore injustice and human suffering. It is simply not the American way of doing things.

❧ We can no longer afford the luxury of a leisurely attack upon prejudice and discrimination. There is much that state and local governments can do in providing positive safeguards for civil rights. But we cannot any longer await the growth of a will to action in the slowest state or the most backward community. Our national government must show the way.

## COMMUNICATING

❧ Never use two words when one will do best.

❧ The simplest words make for the best communication.

❧ I never use $40 words in my language.

❧ I always made it my business to speak plainly and directly to the people without indulging in high-powered oratory.

❧ Listeners have to feel a bond with the speaker; they aren't likely to if they believe he is a "high hat" or "show off." On the other hand, in working for simplicity one has to avoid talking down to an audience.

ꝏ A good speaker genuinely likes people; he respects his listeners.

ꝏ Sometimes I forget the microphone and the formality and really warm up. But you will note it's usually where I want to drive home some important facts and not just phraseology.

ꝏ The greatest orators have been the men who understood what they wanted to say, said it in short sentences and said it quickly and then got out of there before people fell asleep.

CONGRESS

ꝏ If you tell Congress everything about the world situation, they get hysterical. If you tell them nothing, they go fishing.

ꝏ There are liars, trimmers, and pussyfooters on both sides of the aisle in the Senate and the House.

ꝏ Some senators and congressmen come in and pass the time of day and then go out and help me save the world in the press.

ꝏ You can't trust a senator when he can get a headline.

ꝏ Most of the senators who really apply themselves never get much attention in the headlines.

ꝏ I sometimes think that if congressmen talked less and worked more for the public interest they would come out much better and so would the country.

CONVICTION

❧ You don't get any double talk from me. I'm either for something or against it, and you know it. You know what I stand for.

❧ I never sit on a fence. I am either on one side or another.

❧ I have been fiercely partisan in politics and always militantly liberal. I will be that way as long as I live.

❧ I don't like bipartisans. Whenever a fellow tells me he's bipartisan, I know he's going to vote against me.

❧ It takes courage to face a duelist with a pistol and it takes courage to face a British general with an army. But it takes still greater and far higher courage to face friends with a grievance. The bravest thing Andrew Jackson ever did was to stand up and tell his own people to their faces that they were wrong.

CRITICISM

❧ It has not seemed necessary for me to spend a great deal of time calling attention to my mistakes because there have always been plenty of people who were willing to do that for me.

❧ Criticism is something [a president] gets every day, just like breakfast.

❧ It is true that I did not always react pleasantly to criticism—or derisive comments—but I never for a moment questioned the right of anyone to do so.

❧ When they stand up and call you names, it always hurts some, and I don't care how old or how young you are, what age you are.

❧ You have no doubt been at a ballgame when the shortstop would make a home run in an early inning and fail to catch one out in the field later. He is a hero the first time, and they throw pop bottles at him the second time. He needs sympathy in both instances, but seldom gets it, so I never pay any attention to bricks which are thrown my way or to compliments which come my way.

❧ I don't let these things bother me for the simple reason I know that I am trying to do the right thing, and eventually the facts will come out. I'll probably be holding a conference with Saint Peter when that happens.

DECISION MAKING

❧ I don't pass the buck, nor do I alibi out of any decision I make.

❧ It is my duty, as president of the United States, to make the decisions, because I can't pass the buck to anybody; and if I can get all the facts, I have found that the decisions I make as a result of the facts are satisfactory to everybody.

❧ You get all the facts and you make up your mind.

❧ I've always tried to get all the information I could on every job I ever had. So nobody could put anything over on me.

❧ As president, I always insisted on as complete a picture as possible before making a decision, and I did not want fuzzy statements that concealed differences of opinion.

❧ I made it my business as president to listen to people in all walks of life and in all fields of endeavor and experience. I did not see only the people who ought to be seen—that is, those who were "well connected."

I always tried to be a good listener. But since the responsibility for making decisions had to be mine, I always reserved judgment.

I asked members of my staff concerned to submit their recommendations to me in writing. In the evening, I read the staff proposals. Then I went to bed and slept on it. In the morning I made a decision.

Once I had made the decision, I didn't worry over it. If I made a wrong decision, I made another one to correct it.

I was always thinking about what was pending and hoping that the final decision would be correct. I thought about them on my walks. I thought about them in the morning and the afternoon and thought about them after I went to bed and then did a lot of reading to see if I could find some background of history which would affect what had to be done.

If you've had the history and background of the thing that's likely to come up, then after you study all the information you can possibly get, you'll find nine times in ten the decision off the cuff . . . is the correct one.

Looking back, I find that my final decisions usually corresponded to my first "spot decisions."

The most dangerous course a president can follow in a time of crisis is to defer making decisions until they are forced on him and thereupon become inevitable decisions. Events then get out of hand and take control of the president, and he is compelled to overcome situations which he should have prevented.

ꟹ I have never forced myself to think when my energy was low. I simply will not tackle a problem involving an important decision until I feel completely relaxed.

ꟹ I never take a problem to bed with me at night. When I've made a decision, I know it's the best decision I can make under the circumstances and I stop worrying about it.

ꟹ If you are going to walk the floor and worry yourself to death every time you have to make a decision, or if you fail to make up your mind, then you are not suited for the job.

DEMOCRACY

ꟹ Half the fun of being a citizen in this country comes from complaining about the way we run our government—state, federal, and local.

ꟹ No government is perfect. One of the chief virtues of a democracy, however, is that its defects are always visible and under democratic processes can be pointed out and corrected.

ꟹ The people have often made mistakes, but given time and the facts, they will make the corrections.

ꟹ There is no indispensable man in a democracy.

DICTATORSHIP

ꟹ Justice Brandeis used to remark that the separation of powers was not devised to promote efficiency in government. In fact, it was devised to prevent one form of efficiency—absolutism or dictatorship.

❦ Whenever you have an efficient government you have a dictatorship.

❦ A dictatorship is the hardest thing in God's world to hold together because it is made up entirely of conspiracies from the inside.

❦ There is no difference in totalitarian states, call them Nazi, fascist, or communist—they are all the same.

ECONOMICS

❦ It's a recession when your neighbor loses his job; it's a depression when you lose your own.

❦ I was in search of a one-armed economist, so that the guy could never make a statement and then say: "on the other hand."

❦ You know, there's a lot of hooey put out about the budget, but when I was in the White House I understood every item in it.

❦ Budget figures reveal far more about proposed policy than speeches.

❦ More misinformation and plain demagoguery . . . go into the Congressional Record on taxes and the budget than on all other subjects put together.

❦ There is nothing sacred about the pay-as-you-go idea so far as I am concerned, except that it represents the soundest principle of financing that I know.

❧ We believe in economy, and a balanced budget. Therefore, a tax levy should be made to meet the increasing costs of essential security. And the sooner we face up to the need for such a tax, the sooner we will avoid piling up a federal debt that might become unmanageable.

❧ Taxation, in my opinion, should be used for revenue purposes only. While I fought for a more equal distribution of the nation's prosperity among all its citizens, I never advocated taxing the rich to pay the poor. The rate of taxation, to be fair, must be based upon ability to pay. Every social reform which I sponsored was presented in the form of specific legislation, and never in the guise of taxation.

❧ The danger to democracy comes not from the masses but from the concentration of wealth in the hands of a few—and the income tax is the best remedy for that.

❧ [Tight money] reflects a reversion to the idea that the tree can be fertilized at the top instead of the bottom—the old trickle-down theory.

❧ We must never forget that prosperity for other people means prosperity for us and prosperity for us means prosperity for other people.

## EDUCATION

❧ Education is one thing that can't be taken away from you. Nobody can rob you of your education, because that is in your head; that is, if you have any head and are capable of holding it.

❧ It makes not much difference what sort of a building you're in when you're after knowledge, but it does count entirely on who teaches you.

❧ I can remember school teachers, both men and women, who received a stipend for their services but whose ideas consisted of teaching the rising generation that service is much more important than the reward for service. I fear very much that we haven't emphasized that fact enough, although our increasing population, increasing cost of living, and our insane idea of keeping up with the Joneses, has probably had its effect also on the public schools.

❧ I think the fundamental purpose of our educational system is to instill a moral code in the rising generation and create a citizenship which will be responsible for the welfare of the nation.

## ETHICS

❧ Since a child at my mother's knee, I have believed in honor, ethics, and right living as its own reward.

❧ If I think it is right, I am going to do it.

❧ It's like old Mark Twain said, "Always do right. This will gratify some people and astonish the rest."

❧ Wrongdoers have no house with me.

❧ I can always get along with an honest man.

❧ There are honorable men in all walks of life; in fact honest men far outnumber the men of sharp practice.

❧ Do your duty and history will do you justice.

FINE ARTS

❧ I know nothing about Art with a capital A, particularly the frustrated brand known as Modern.

❧ I dislike Picasso, and all the moderns—they are lousy. Any kid can take an egg and a piece of ham and make more understandable pictures.

❧ Did you ever sit and listen to an orchestra play a fine overture and imagine that things were as they ought to be and not as they are? Music that I can understand always makes me feel that way.

❧ I don't like what passes for music today. Maybe I'm old-fashioned. I like something with a tune or melody to it.

FITNESS

❧ You can't be mentally fit unless you're physically fit.

❧ After you are fifty years old, [walking] is the best exercise you can take. Of course, some aging exhibitionists try to prove that they can play tennis or handball or anything else they did when they were eighteen. And every once in a while one of them falls dead of a heart attack. I say that's not for me.

❧ If you are going to walk for your physical benefit, it is necessary that you walk as if you are going some place. If you walk 120 paces a minute, your whole body gets a vigorous workout. You swing your arms and take deep breaths as you walk.

ൾ I walk and swim and worry very little. I appoint people to responsible positions to worry for me. You have no idea how satisfactory that policy is.

ൾ All my life I've been relatively free from worry, and maybe that's the best formula for long life.

GOVERNMENT

ൾ I think we have the greatest government the world has ever seen. The more I become familiar with it, the better I like it, even if it does make a slave out of the president.

ൾ We have the greatest republic in the world if we remember that the people elect us to do what we think is right and not what some pollster or misguided editorial writer tells us to do.

ൾ The least government is the best government. We should have just as little as we can get along with.

ൾ It has been my experience in public life that there are few problems which cannot be worked out, if we make a real effort to understand the other fellow's point of view, and if we try to find a solution on the basis of give-and-take, of fairness to both sides.

ൾ I think one of the reasons for the lack of interest in the right to vote is fundamentally due to plain laziness and the idea of letting George do it. Voters who claim they have no hand in the selection of candidates or those who take no interest in the political party are like a great many people who do not like to take responsibility themselves but who find it much more pleasant to find fault with those who are willing to take the responsibility.

We would help to cure senility and seniority—both terrible legislative diseases nationally—if twelve years were the limit of service for president, senator, and congressman.

The convention system has its faults, of course, but I do not know of a better method for choosing a presidential nominee.

I am against presidential state primaries, because a man cannot stand two strenuous campaigns—one to win the state primaries and another to run for election.

A national presidential primary would force a candidate to raise a huge sum of money in order to tour the country and make his good points known. No poor man or even one fairly well fixed could finance a national campaign. The money would have to be raised and contributed by the wealthy and the special interests. The nominee would become obligated to contributors, and that would not be good for the country.

HEALTH CARE

When we find that 34% of our young men and women are unfit for military service because of physical and mental defects, there is something wrong with the health of the country and I am trying to find a remedy for it.

I am trying to fix it so the people in the middle-income bracket can live as long as the very rich and the very poor.

I usually find that those who are loudest in protesting against medical help by the federal government are those who do not need help.

ꟹ I have had some bitter disappointments as president, but the one that has troubled me most, in a personal way, has been the failure to defeat organized opposition to a national compulsory health insurance program.

HIMSELF

ꟹ I'm just a politician from Missouri and proud of it.

ꟹ I'm a meat and potatoes man.

ꟹ I've been one of the worst customers the sleeping pill manufacturers ever had.

ꟹ I like to gossip with friends. I like to exchange views and opinion with people in all walks of life.

ꟹ I like people and I like to be among them.

ꟹ I'm a damned sentimentalist who is contrary as hell in fundamental things, but who can be deeply touched on a personal basis.

ꟹ I could hardly hold my voice steady when I gave a medal to a widow or a father for heroism in action.

ꟹ I have been accused of quick temper. I prefer to think that I am quick to retort when provoked on a sensitive issue. But, having once expressed myself and made my position clear, I harbor no vengeful or bitter feelings toward anyone.

ꟹ I used to watch my father and mother closely to learn what I could do to please them, just as I did with my schoolteachers and playmates. Because of my efforts to get along with my associates I usually was able to get what I wanted.

❧ If my mother knew my position on civil rights she would have "disinherited me." My mother died unreconstructed.

❧ There was never one of our name who had sense enough to make money. I am no exception.

❧ It's been my policy to do every job assigned to me just a little better than anyone else has done it.

❧ I never ran for a political office I wanted. But I've fought for every one I've ever had. Damn it! I've never had an office I didn't have to fight for, tooth or nail.

❧ I have always said that if I ever caught a fellow that was trying to shoot me, I would stick a gun down his throat and pull the trigger.

❧ I'm not a scholar. I know I read the wrong books, but I read a lot, and I suppose I got some good ones now and then.

❧ If I couldn't have been a pianist, I think I would have done better as a professor of history.

HISTORY

❧ While still a boy I could see that history had some extremely valuable lessons to teach.

❧ There is nothing new in the world except the history you do not know.

You must know the historical background of what makes the world go 'round. After all, there is little real change in the problems of government from the beginnings of time down to the present. Those problems today are just about the same as they were for Mesopotamia and Egypt, for the Hittites, for Greece and Rome, for Carthage and Great Britain and France.

Most of the problems a president has to face have their roots in the past.

Our American political situation is about the same from generation to generation. The main difficulty is that the rising generation never knows about the acts of the previous one—most people think it too much trouble to find out.

Men make history. History does not make the man.

## HUMAN NATURE

In reading the lives of great men, I found that the first victory they won was over themselves and their carnal urges. Self discipline with all of them came first.

There are always weak people in every human setup. The human animal is built that way. When the golden apple is dangled before them, some take a bite out of it, and some eat the whole apple.

Men often mistake notoriety for fame, and would rather be remarked for their vices and follies than not be noticed at all.

There is a lure in power. It can get into a man's blood just as gambling and lust for money have been known to do.

When an egotist is punctured, a lot of noise and whistling always accompanies the escaping air.

All of us have a very deep sentimental streak in us, but most of the time we are too timid or too contrary to show it.

Happiness is a state of mind. A farmhand, if he has an ample living, can be just as happy as a millionaire with homes in Maine and Florida.

There's nothing new in human nature; only our names for things change.

The human animal has not changed very much. He has to be guided in the proper direction under a moral code, and then there must be some machinery to make him live within that moral code.

The human animal and his emotions change not much from age to age. He must change now or he faces absolute and complete destruction and maybe the insect age or an atmosphereless planet will succeed him.

Our tribal instinct has not been eliminated by science and invention. We, as individuals, haven't caught up physically or ethically with the atomic age. Will we?

HUMAN RELATIONS

Always be nice to all the people who can't talk back to you. I can't stand a man or woman who bawls out underlings to satisfy an ego.

Haven't you ever been overawed by a secretary and finally, when you have reached the man you wanted to see, discovered he was very human?

About the meanest thing you can say about a man [is] that he means well.

INTERNATIONAL RELATIONS

International relations have traditionally been compared to a chess game in which each nation tries to outwit and checkmate the other.

No nation on this globe should be more internationally minded than America because it was built by all nations.

Isolationism is the road to war. Worse than that, isolationism is the road to defeat in war.

No country is so remote from us that it may not some day be involved in a matter which threatens the peace. Remember that the First World War began in Serbia; that the peace of Versailles was first broken in Manchuria; and that the Second World War began in Poland. Who knows what may happen in the future? Our foreign policy must be universal.

I don't believe in [summit conferences]. They don't amount to a damn. I have been to two of them, and nothing was accomplished.

The CIA was set up by me for the sole purpose of getting all the available information to the president. It was not intended to operate as an international agency engaged in strange activities.

Americans are funny birds. They are always sticking their noses into somebody's business which isn't any of theirs. We send missionaries and political propagandists to China, Turkey, India, and everywhere to tell those people how to live. Most of 'em know as much or more than we do.

We in America always think of China as a nation. But the truth is that in 1945 China was only a geographical expression.

In all the history of the world we are the first great nation to create independent republics from conquered territory, Cuba and the Philippines. Our neighbors are not afraid of us. Their borders have no forts, no soldiers, no tanks, no big guns lined up.

I have never approved of the practice of the strong imposing their will on the weak, whether among men or nations.

All sorts of people make up this world, and there are about 3 billion people in the world, and only about 900 million that are white. You have to get along with the rest of them or you will be overwhelmed.

The top dog in a world which is 90 percent colored ought to clean his own house.

LEADERSHIP

You can't breed or teach leadership: it comes naturally.

Not all readers become leaders. But all leaders must be readers.

A successful leader cannot afford to lose the common touch.

He's using his head if he talks to everyone in sight and listens to everyone and listens hard. . . . You'll find that the willingness to talk to people is true of all the great men in our history.

My definition of a leader in a free country is a man who can persuade people to do what they don't want to do and like it.

Leadership is the art of getting other people to run with your idea as if it were their own.

I am willing and want to pass the credit around. The objective is the thing, not personal aggrandizement.

Keep working on a plan. Make no little plans. Make the biggest one you can think of, and spend the rest of your life carrying it out.

You can always amend a big plan, but you can never expand a little one. I don't believe in little plans. I believe in plans big enough to meet a situation which we can't possibly foresee now.

It is the job of any administrator to know how to judge men. I don't care whether he works in a packing house, a newspaper, or a bank or in government—it's all the same.

## MARRIAGE

❧ I don't like divorces because I think that when you make a contract, you should keep it. The marriage contract is one of the most sacred in the world.

❧ A man not honorable in his marital relations is not usually honorable in any other.

❧ When a man gets the right kind of wife, his career is made—and I got just that.

## THE MILITARY

❧ [The armed forces] do a good job on the waste side. They throw money around by the scoop shovelful.

❧ If there is one basic element in our constitution, it is civilian control of the military. Politics are to be made by the elected political officials, not by generals or admirals.

❧ One reason that we have been so careful to keep the military within its own preserve is that the very nature of the service hierarchy gives military commanders little if any opportunity to learn the humility that is needed for good public service.

❧ The professional soldier is educated in an institution that creates the idea that an officer in the Army is better than the private, the corporal, and the sergeant, and when he becomes the chief executive, he can't get it out of his mind that he's way above everybody else in intelligence and character and everything.

They're honorable men. They want to do the right thing, but they've been educated in a manner that's like a horse with blinders on—he sees only one direction right down the road.

All the generals like flattery.

Most generals have the idea that as commanding generals they're going to retire someday to a nice post and sit there and wait for their term to end, and some of them think they can retire to the White House as commander in chief and do the same thing.

The only military hero who really made a good president was George Washington, and he was not really a professional soldier.

I think history has proven that professional military men have trouble running a free government. Because the professional military man is used most of the time to being a dictator.

[Eisenhower:] He'll sit here, and he'll say, "Do this! Do that!" And nothing will happen. Poor Ike—it won't be a bit like the Army.

The air boys are for glamor and the Navy as always is the greatest of propaganda machines.

The Marine Corps is the Navy's police force and as long as I am president that is what it will remain. They have a propaganda machine that is almost equal to Stalin's.

I know how [soldiers] are, they are trained not to give up. I know because I am one of them.

## MISCELLANEY

❧ One of the bravest and one of the best soldiers was Uriah. But the quality of the name Uriah has been ruined because Charles Dickens created a character named Uriah Heep, a sniveling hypocrite.

❧ I don't give a damn about ["The Missouri Waltz"] but I can't say it out loud because it's the song of Missouri. It's as bad as "The Star-Spangled Banner" so far as music is concerned.

❧ They [the FBI] are dabbling in sex life scandals and plain blackmail when they should be catching criminals.

❧ [Autograph seekers are] like pups who see a fire plug.

❧ [Souvenir hunters are] just people who want to accumulate a lot of stuff and then throw it away. You find most of it in the attic when they die.

❧ I've found that critics usually are picked from frustrated people who have made a failure in the things they criticize.

❧ An economist is a man who wears a watch chain with a Phi Beta Kappa key at one end and no watch at the other.

❧ A consultant is an ordinary citizen away from home.

❧ Dignitaries are much more ideal in print than face to face.

❧ California crackpots are the most incongruous people. They come from Iowa, Nebraska, Kansas, and, I'm sorry to say, our own good State of Missouri. They join such outfits as the one headed by Aimee Semple McPherson, Yoga and any other nut set-up a good salesman starts.

[Nevada:] That awful, sinful place . . . which should never have been made a state.

NATIONALITIES

It was said in the First World War that the French fought for their country, the British fought for freedom of the seas, and the Americans fought for souvenirs.

The ancestor worshipers who stayed in England, France, and Spain did not make the western hemisphere great. It was the so-called lower classes who wanted to improve their lot who made North and South America and Australia and New Zealand great.

The Chinese, as you know, are fundamentally anti-foreign, and we must be exceedingly careful to see that this anti-foreign sentiment is not turned in our direction.

Russians distribute lies about us. Our papers lie about and misrepresent the motives of the Russians—and the British outlie and outpropagandize us both.

Russia is a great country and the Soviet Union is made up of sturdy people but they have been oppressed and downtrodden by dictatorships from the time of Ivan the Terrible and Peter the Great to this very day.

[The Russians] are tough bargainers and always ask for the whole earth, expecting maybe to get an acre.

You never saw such pig-headed people as are the Russians. I hope I never have to hold another conference with them.

## NATIVE AMERICANS

Many of the Indians were inclined to be friendly to the whites and were perfectly willing to make treaties with them. But the attitude of the white settlers from Europe was that the Indians were savages and an inferior race, and therefore the settlers had a perfect right to chase them off the land and take it away from them, which is what we did eventually.

The treatment of the Indians by the white settlers of both South America and North America was a disgrace and always will be.

How would I mark our paper in terms of the Indian? Zero minus.

There were several men who tried their best to do justice to the Indians, but they didn't have much of a chance because the crooks were always standing at the door ready to take what was loose.

The Indians didn't understand the approach of the white man in business dealings, and they got cheated every time they got into a trade with the white man.

They weren't an inferior race at all, of course. They were wonderfully wise people, and there were Indian setups in the western hemisphere that were almost ideal systems of government.

Some of the greatest leaders this country ever produced were the leaders of the Indian tribes.

I have always felt that the Indians should have been allowed to maintain themselves on the lands and improve their position, and eventually would have become friendly to us. They had the same sort of brains and body as we have, and they are a brave people.

## OLD AGE

❧ As you get older, you get tired of doing the same things over and over again, so you think Christmas has changed. It hasn't. It's you who has changed.

❧ It is remarkable indeed how time flies and makes you an old man whether you want to be or not.

❧ At 79 you go to funeral after funeral of your friends, most of whom are younger than 79—and you sometimes wonder if the old man with the scythe isn't after you.

❧ I don't like . . . to be called a "senior citizen." I still get around and when I get to be a "senior citizen" I hope they will put me in a pine box and cover me up.

## PEACE

❧ I'd rather have lasting peace in the world than be president. I wish for peace, I work for peace, and I pray for peace continually.

❧ We must find a way to peace, or else civilization will be destroyed and the world will turn back to the year 900.

❧ We must face the fact that peace must be built upon power, as well as upon good will and good deeds.

❧ It only takes one nation to make war. But it takes two or more to make a peace.

❧ I don't believe that because peace is difficult that war is inevitable.

We can well afford to pay the price of peace. Our only alternate is to pay the terrible cost of war.

PERSONAL PREFERENCES

I've got other things to do besides watch television.

I never had enough money to play golf.

I've never had a hobby in my life.

I have never cared for air conditioning for myself, preferring fresh air no matter how hot or cold.

My favorite animal is the mule. He has a lot more horse sense than a horse. He knows when to stop eating. And he knows when to stop working.

Most people don't know when the best part of the day is: it's the early morning.

PHILOSOPHY

I am inclined to attribute my good health, and that of my family, primarily to our outlook on life, and to our philosophical approach to other people and to ourselves.

I grew up to look for the good in people. I have never regarded people with suspicion—for such an attitude usually leads to worrying yourself into being a pessimist about everything, people included.

I have never seen pessimists make anything work, or contribute anything of lasting value.

ɛʊ̃ You must watch out for these people who make mountains out of something that doesn't exist—not even a molehill!

ɛʊ̃ Three things can ruin a man: power, money, and women. I never wanted power, I never had any money, and the only woman in my life is up at the house right now.

ɛʊ̃ I don't care what your politics are, I don't care what you believe politically, and I don't care what your religion is, as long as you live by it and act by it.

ɛʊ̃ Do your best, history will do the rest.

POLITICAL INTEGRITY

ɛʊ̃ Lies, slander, mud-slinging are the weapons of the totalitarians. No man of morals or ethics will use them.

ɛʊ̃ Politics force men into contacts with all manner of people, but men of principle need never surrender them in order to gain or to hold political office.

ɛʊ̃ Wherever you find a crooked politician, you'll find a crooked businessman behind him.

ɛʊ̃ An honest public servant can't become rich in politics.

ɛʊ̃ I would have nothing to do with money. I just wouldn't handle it. I wouldn't collect it, I wouldn't distribute it, I wouldn't have anything in the world to do with it.

ɛʊ̃ I would much rather be an honorable public servant and known as such than to be the richest man in the world.

POLITICAL PARTIES

I think we would lose something important to our political life if the conservatives were all in one party and the liberals in the other. This would make us a nation divided either into two opposing and irreconcilable camps or into even smaller and contentious groups, such as have plagued recent European history.

There is no need for a third party, since our two-party system has made our country strong and politically responsive. All segments of our economy and society have adequate representation and expression within either or both parties.

Never in the history of any free country has there been a time when one party could run that country forever. Because opposition is good for any party.

[The Democratic Party] is the party of the common people, whereas the Republican Party is the party of special privilege.

The Republicans prefer to leave the power in the hands of the special interests rather than the man in the White House.

When a leader is in the Democratic Party he's a boss. When he's in the Republican Party he's nothing but a leader. But there's no difference.

When I hear Republicans say I'm doing all right, I know damned well I'm doing wrong.

A sound government to the Republican is the kind of government where the president makes nice sounds while the vice-president snarls.

Republicans don't like people to talk about depressions. You remember the old saying: "Don't talk about rope in the house of somebody who has to be hanged."

The Republicans have General Motors and General Electric and General Foods and General MacArthur . . . every general I know is on this list except general welfare, and general welfare is in with the corporals and privates in the Democratic Party.

The Republican Party either corrupts its liberals or it expels them.

## POLITICIANS

I'm proud to be a politician. A politician is a man who understands government, and it takes a politician to run a government.

A statesman is a politician who's been dead 10 or 15 years.

A great politician is known by the service he renders. He doesn't have to become president or governor or the head of his city or county to be a great politician. There are mayors of villages, county attorneys, county commissioners or supervisors who render just as great service locally as do the heads of the government.

There are more honest men who are professional politicians than there are honest bankers and businessmen. The word of a successful man in politics is worth more than the bond of a banker, or a big businessman.

The difficulty with businessmen entering politics, after they have had a successful business career, is that they want to start at the top.

You can tell a good politician by how sincere he is in liking and wanting to help people.

If you don't like people, you hadn't ought to be in politics at all.

I think there comes a time when every politician, whether he be in a county, state, or federal office, should retire. Most of them find it impossible to do that—they either have to be carried out feet first or kicked out.

Many of us have been licked many a time because the people thought that another man was better and it's good for us; it keeps us from getting a big head.

There is no conversation so sweet as that of former political enemies.

### POLITICS

Politics is a fascinating game, because politics is government. It is the art of government.

Politics is . . . a game of people and how they will act under certain conditions. You never can tell, but you can sometimes guess and I've been a good guesser.

I have always defined politics to mean the science of government, perhaps the most important science, because it involves the art and ability of people to live together.

Politics is the ability to get along with people, and politics is government, and some of the so called bosses are just people who understand the political situation from the ground up.

ǽ If you are for it, it is statesmanlike. If you are against it, it is purely low politics!

ǽ Politics—good politics—is public service. There is no life or occupation in which a man can find a greater opportunity to serve his community or his country.

## POLLS

ǽ I wonder how far Moses would have gone if he'd taken a poll in Egypt? What would Jesus Christ have preached if he'd taken a poll in the land of Israel? Where would the Reformation have gone if Martin Luther had taken a poll?

ǽ It isn't polls or public opinion of the moment that counts. It's right and wrong and leadership—men with fortitude, honesty, and a belief in the right that make epochs in the history of the world.

ǽ A man who is influenced by the polls or is afraid to make decisions which may make him unpopular is not a man to represent the welfare of the country.

## THE PRESIDENCY

ǽ The presidency is the most peculiar office in the history of the world.

ǽ The presidency will make a man out of any boy.

ǽ Being a president is like riding a tiger. A man has to keep on riding or be swallowed.

I do not know of any easy way to be president. It is more than a full-time job, and the relaxations are few.

No president ever had any real rest!

Lincoln had fits of melancholy. . . . Melancholy goes with the job.

To be president of the United States is to be lonely, very lonely at times of great decisions.

The greatest part of the president's job is to make decisions—big ones and small ones, dozens of them almost every day. The papers may circulate around the government for a while but they finally reach his desk. And then, there's no place else for them to go. The president—whoever he is—has to decide. He can't pass the buck to anybody. No one else can do the deciding for him. That's his job.

Presidents have to make decisions if they're going to get anywhere, and those presidents who couldn't make decisions are the ones who caused all the trouble.

The United States has never suffered seriously from any acts of the president that were intended for the welfare of the country. It's suffered from the inaction of a great many presidents when actions should have been taken at the right time.

First, he should be an honorable man. Then he should be a man who can get elected. Finally, he should be a man who knows what to do after he is elected.

ꕥ You have to know something to be a president. You have got to be a jack-of-all-trades and know something about all of them.

ꕥ It's almost impossible for a man to be president of the United States without learning something.

ꕥ Any man who sincerely tries to live up to the responsibilities of the office cannot keep from growing in the presidency.

ꕥ If you don't have a good sense of humor, you're in a hell of a fix when you are president of the United States.

ꕥ The president of the United States is two people—he's the president and he's a human being. The president has to spend half his time keeping the human being in line, and, at that, he doesn't do a very good job of it.

ꕥ He has more duties and powers than a Roman emperor, a general, a Hitler, or a Mussolini; but he never uses those powers or prerogatives, because he is a democrat (with a little "d") and because he believes in the Magna Carta and the Bill of Rights.

ꕥ A good president has to be a man—or as of course will come in time, a woman—who works for the people in a way that makes a great impression on the period in which he lives.

ꕥ I've said for a long time that women have everything else, they might as well have the presidency.

ꕥ County judge, chairman of a committee, president of the United States. They are all the same kind of jobs. It is the business of dealing with people.

The president spends most of his time kissing people first on one cheek and then on the other in order to get them to do what they ought to do without getting kissed.

He is the number-one public relations man of the government.

If a president isn't in an occasional fight with the Congress or the courts, he's not doing a good job.

A man with thin skin has no business being president.

A president cannot always be popular. He has to be able to say *yes* and *no,* and more often *no.*

A strong president can't avoid controversy, and shouldn't, either. The more controversy you have, the better it is for the big issues, because then the president can go before the public and explain what the people who are against him stand for and what he stands for.

A man in his right mind would never want to be president if he knew what it entails. Aside from the impossible administrative burden, he has to take all sorts of abuse from liars and demagogues.

A president may dismiss the abuse of scoundrels, but to be denounced by honest men honestly outraged is a test of greatness that none but the strongest men survive.

The president of the United States hears a hundred voices telling him that he is the greatest man in the world. He must listen carefully indeed to hear the one voice that tells him he is not.

❧ Anybody can be president, and, when he reaches the end of his term, he can go back to being anybody again. It's the job that counts, not the man.

THE PRESIDENCY OF HARRY TRUMAN

❧ I've never taken an attitude that the kudos and kow-tows are made to me as an individual. I knew always that the greatest office in the history of the world was getting them, and Harry S. Truman as an individual was not.

❧ In the White House, I never allowed myself to think that Harry Truman from Independence, Missouri, was a person deciding the fate of the world. I was deciding as president, and not as an individual thinking in terms of what he would prefer as an individual.

❧ Nobody but a damn fool would have the job in the first place. But I've got it damn fool or no and I have to do it as best I can.

❧ I am in a position that's too big for me. In fact I think it's too big for anybody but I know it's too big for me. I need help, help, help.

❧ The president can't cross the street without creating an incident. But this president likes to create incidents.

❧ I think the proper thing to do and the thing I have been doing, is to do what I think is right and let them all go to hell.

I sign my name, on the average, 600 times a day, see and talk to hundreds of people every month, shake hands with thousands every year, and still carry on the business of the largest going concern in the whole world.

I am the hired man of one hundred and fifty million people and it is a job that keeps me right busy.

It seems that there's somebody for supper every night.

There are probably hundreds of people better qualified than I am to be president, but they weren't elected.

Adlai [Stevenson], if a knucklehead like me can be president and not do too badly, think what a really educated smart guy like you could do in the job.

Some of the presidents were great and some of them weren't. I can say that, because I wasn't one of the great presidents, but I had a good time trying to be one, I can tell you that.

I have tried my best to give the nation everything I had in me. . . . I always quote one epitaph which is on a tombstone in the cemetery in Tombstone, Arizona. It says, "Here lies Jack Williams. He done his damndest." I think that is the greatest epitaph that a man can have.

## THE PRESIDENT'S FAMILY AND ASSOCIATES

The White House is a difficult place to raise a family, and the environment is not always a normal atmosphere for an American child.

❧ I have often thought that those presidents who did not have any children suffered less embarrassment in certain things than those that did have them.

❧ I do not know whether presidents ought to have any descendants, because their descendants inherit the difficult burden of having people expect them to live up to their ancestors.

❧ There is something awesome about the head of the United States—not me, but the presidency itself—that causes people to become disturbed and rattled when they are around him. I just have to think back to my first interview with President Roosevelt and I know exactly how they feel.

❧ It would be a terrible thing for the president in his office to seem discourteous through lack of warmth to people who come to see him, because it hurts, and people never get over being hurt. I try my best to remember that at all times.

❧ I'd say that 96 percent of the men and women around most presidents are good people.

❧ It's hell when a man gets in close association with the president. Something happens to him.

❧ A yes-man on the White House staff or in the cabinet is worthless!

❧ I do not like this present trend toward a huge White House staff. . . . A layer of presidential aides has been placed between the president and his appointed officials. Mostly, these aides get in one another's way. They tend to insulate the president. The president needs breathing space. The smaller the staff around him, the better.

THE PRESIDENT IN RETIREMENT

❧ Two hours ago I could have said five words and been quoted in fifteen minutes in every capital in the world. Now I could talk for two hours and nobody would give a damn.

❧ I am now in the army of unemployed presidents. But it is a very small army.

❧ I still don't feel like a completely private citizen and I don't suppose I ever will. It's still almost impossible to do as other people do, even though I've tried.

❧ You can't sit in the sun like other old men do.

❧ They are trying to make an elder statesman of me but they will never succeed.

THE PRESS

❧ If you have a free press, there's no way in the world for anyone to get by with the subversion of the government.

❧ The objective of the press is to sell papers and advertising, and you should always keep that in mind.

❧ Lies and mud make "news"—the truth and flowers do not.

❧ If you want to get a headline all you need to do is fall out with some of your friends, and you will always get it.

ꕥ Our means of communicating and consolidating public opinion—the press and the radio—emphasize the differences of opinion rather than agreements. A president must not be influenced by this distortion of opinion. He must be able to distinguish between propaganda and the true opinion of the people.

ꕥ The press is conditioned by its movements in the day-to-day news and issues—and has not managed to develop a sense of the future.

ꕥ I've always . . . had a lot more faith in poets than in reporters. Reporters just tell what has happened, and they don't do too good a job of it a lot of the time, but poets, some of them, they write about what's going to happen.

ꕥ You should never form judgments from front page headlines. As with a contract, the fine print on the inside pages should be carefully studied.

ꕥ No man who is in a place of responsibility can pay any attention to what the editors of the papers have to say about him. If he does, he'll never have a policy.

ꕥ It makes no difference what the papers say if you are right.

ꕥ When you read what the press had to say about Washington, Jefferson, and Lincoln, and the other presidents, you would think that we never had a decent man in the office since the country began.

ꕥ When the press stops abusing me, I'll know I'm in the wrong pew.

I never cared anything about what the newspapers said about me as long as they didn't jump on my family, and then they got in trouble.

I have been told that when a fellow fails at everything else, he either starts a hotel or a newspaper.

Editors are peculiar animals—they throw mud and bricks at you the whole year round—then they make one favorable statement which happens to agree with facts and they think they should be hugged and kissed for it.

They are always for a man when he is winning, but when he is in a little trouble, they all jump on him with what ought to be done, which they didn't tell him before.

I find in my dealings with distinguished newspapermen they are all thin skinned—they like to give a public man hell but when he comes back a little, they find it hard to take.

In the picture *Mr. Smith Goes to Washington* it was perfectly all right to show senators as either silly or as crooks but when the show put on a drunken newspaper reporter in his true character, it killed the picture.

To hell with them. When history is written they will be the sons of bitches—not I.

I'm saving up four or five good, hard punches on the nose, and when I'm out of this job, I'm going to run around and deliver them personally [to members of the press].

## RELIGION

❧ All the religion I have is found in the Ten Commandments and the Sermon on the Mount.

❧ If men and nations would but live by the precepts of the ancient prophets and the teachings of the Sermon on the Mount, problems which now seem so difficult would soon disappear.

❧ Material things are ashes, if there is no spiritual background for the support of those material things.

❧ I myself always thought there were plenty of doors to heaven and don't think you have to go through any single one, although I thought the Baptist was most likely to get there.

❧ I'm a Baptist because I think that sect gives the common man the shortest and most direct approach to God. I've never thought the Almighty is greatly interested in pomp and circumstance.

❧ Those who resorted to wars to inflict their kind of Christianity upon other faiths or denominations did not really understand Christianity.

❧ I rather think there is an immense shortage of Christian charity among so-called Christians.

❧ Who is to blame for present conditions but sniveling church members who weep on Sunday, play with whores on Monday, drink on Tuesday, sell out to the Boss on Wednesday, repent about Friday, and start over on Sunday.

My Grandfather Young once told me, "When a man spends Saturday night and Sunday doing too much howling and praying, you had better go home and lock your smoke house."

Religious stuffed shirts are just as bad or worse than political ones in my opinion.

I've always believed that religion is something to live by and not to talk about.

I've come to the conclusion myself that church is a very handy place to have a nap in most instances.

ROOTS

I can remember how our Kentucky relatives used to hold their heads high and their noses up when they came to see us poor Missourians. They've changed somewhat since one of those poor relations . . . became the president of the United States.

My home town, Independence, the County Seat of Jackson County, Missouri, is in my opinion the best place for a retired Missouri farmer to live. That state has had three "notorious" characters—Mark Twain, Jesse James, and myself. The other two are shoveling coal for Pluto and I'm all that's left to appear for them.

I've had every political office, nearly, from precinct to president of the United States, and I came back home to live at the end of it all.

☙ A man should be buried where his home is, where he belongs.

THE VICE PRESIDENCY

☙ A president was going over detailed matters of state with his staff. Happening to glance out the window just as the vice president sauntered by the White House, he said, "There goes the vice president, with nothing on his mind but the health of the president."

☙ There's an old joke that the vice president's principal chore is to get up in the morning and ask how the president is feeling.

☙ The vice president simply presides over the Senate and sits around hoping for a funeral.

☙ I bet I can go down on the street and stop the first ten men I see and that they can't tell me the names of two of the last ten vice presidents of the United States.

☙ Jefferson was a bit bored as vice president because he often felt he just didn't have enough to do, and I'm in sympathy with that feeling because I felt that way myself once or twice when I had the job.

☙ Do you remember your American history well enough to recall what happened to most vice presidents who succeeded to the presidency? Usually they were ridiculed in office, had their hearts broken, lost any vestige of respect they had had before.

## WAR

❦ Starting a war is no way to make peace.

❦ I have always been opposed even to the thought of fighting a "preventive war." There is nothing more foolish than to think that war can be stopped by war. You don't "prevent" anything by war except peace.

❦ The one purpose that dominated me in everything I thought and did [as president] was to prevent a third world war.

❦ I was a soldier in the First World War, and I know what a soldier goes through. I know well the anguish that mothers and fathers and families go through.

❦ I hate war. War destroys individuals and whole generations. It throws civilization into the dark ages.

❦ Warfare, no matter what weapons it employs, is a means to an end, and if that end can be achieved by negotiated settlements of conditional surrender, there is no need for war.

❦ Victorious nations cannot, on the surrender of a vicious and dangerous enemy, turn their backs and go home. Wars are different from baseball games where, at the end of the game, the teams get dressed and leave the park.

❦ We have found that the victor loses in total war as well as the vanquished.

❦ If we do not abolish war on this earth, then surely one day, war will abolish us from the earth.

WASHINGTON, D.C.

❧ Rumors are always circulating in Washington. It wouldn't be a good town if it weren't for the rumors.

❧ If you want a friend in Washington, buy a dog.

❧ There are more prima donnas per square foot in public life here in Washington than in all the opera companies ever to exist.

❧ Woodrow Wilson said that a great many men came to Washington and grew with their jobs, and a very large number came and just swelled up.

❧ I have had all of Washington that I want.

# *Harry Truman's Life Stories*

## PRECOCITY

Harry Truman's earliest memory was of chasing a frog when he was two. Every time the frog jumped, Harry laughed uproariously. He remembered hearing his grandfather tell his mother, "It's very strange that a two-year-old has such a sense of humor."

## DAD

When an interviewer suggested that Truman's father—who lost all his money speculating—was a failure, the president bristled. "My father was not a failure," he said. "After all, he was the father of a president of the United States."

## COLONEL CRISP

Truman's family sometimes spent summer days at Democratic picnics. A frequent orator at these events was a perennial candidate for Congress named Colonel Crisp. Crisp's favorite oration depicted the Civil War Battle of Lone Jack. A veteran of that battle once challenged the speaker's veracity. As Truman loved to recall, Crisp responded, "Goddamn an eyewitness anyway. He always spoils a good story."

## YOUNG REPUBLICANS

In 1892, when Grover Cleveland was running for president and Adlai Stevenson for vice president on the Democratic ticket, six-year-old Harry wore a campaign hat to school that read CLEVELAND AND STEVENSON. Some Republican classmates grabbed the cap from his head, then tore it up. "And the Republicans have been trying to do that to me ever since," Truman said years later.

## FOUR-EYES

Truman's thick eyeglasses kept him from playing ball or rough-housing with other boys. Instead, Harry tried to read his way through the local library. As a result, he got called "bookworm," "sissy," and "four-eyes." But the gift of good eyesight was worth the taunts. "When I first put the glasses on," Truman recalled, "I saw things and saw print I'd never seen before. I learned to read when I was five but never could see the fine print. I've been 'fine printed' many a time since I've been able to read it."

## CHILDHOOD SWEETHEART

During Sunday school at the First Presbyterian Church, Harry saw someone he later described as "a very beautiful little lady with lovely blue eyes and the prettiest golden curls I've ever seen." This was Elizabeth Virginia "Bessie" Wallace, to whom he'd eventually be married for fifty-three years. "I was smitten at once," Truman later said of their first meeting, "and still am."

A STRAIGHT PLOWER

Truman's mother, Martha—who referred to herself as a "light-foot" Baptist—always advised her son to be good, but not too good. When Harry was elected to the Senate, Martha Truman told reporters, "I knew that boy would amount to something from the time he was nine years old. He could plow the straightest row of corn in the county."

TENDING BAR

Before and after high school, Truman worked at Clinton's Drugstore. The owner kept bottles of whiskey behind his prescription case. One of Harry's tasks was to set them up. Every morning a steady stream of local citizens—including prominent church members and Anti-Saloon League activists—ducked behind the prescription case for a dram of "medicine." Dropping a dime on the counter, they'd wipe their mouths, glance through the peephole, and slip out the door. "There were saloons aplenty around the square in Independence," Truman wrote in his memoirs, "and many leading men in town made no bones about going into them and buying a drink. I learned to think more highly of them than I did of the prescription-counter drinkers."

WORTHY OF A KISS

Truman was a good student in high school, but not the best. His friend Charlie Ross was valedictorian of their senior class and edited its yearbook. At their graduation in 1901, Ross was given a kiss by their English teacher, Matilda "Tillie" Brown. Ross's classmates protested this favoritism. Miss Brown stood firm. Whoever earned a kiss, she said, would get one. After Truman became president over four decades later, he hired Ross as his press secretary. The first person they called to tell about it was Tillie Brown. "Miss Brown," Truman told her, "this is the president of the United States. Do I get that kiss?"

## AGRICULTURAL SCIENCE

After high school Truman spent what he later called the best ten years of his life working on his family's six-hundred-acre farm. Truman regarded farming as good training for a future man of affairs. "I thought of Cincinnatus and a lot of other farm boys who had made good," he explained, "and I thought maybe by cussing mules and plowing corn I could perhaps overcome my shyness and amount to something."

## PREPARING FOR THE PRESIDENCY

"I don't suppose I'd ever have been real pleased if I hadn't tried just once to get rich quickly," Harry told Bess. His most ambitious stab involved drilling for oil near Eureka, Kansas. When they reached nine hundred feet without a strike, he and his partners sold their lease. The company that bought it struck oil a few hundred feet deeper throughout the 320-acre site. This company later became Cities Service. Had Truman's group kept drilling, they would have become millionaires. His entire life would then have been very different. As Truman later speculated from the White House, "Maybe I wouldn't be Pres if we'd hit."

## A LATE PROPOSAL

In 1917, Bess accepted one of Harry's many proposals of marriage. He was thirty-four, she thirty-three. When Truman enlisted in the Army, the two postponed their wedding. "I didn't think it was right to get married and maybe come home a cripple and have the most beautiful and sweetest girl in the world tied down," he explained.

## THOROUGHLY SCARED

Truman was promoted to captain and appointed commander of an artillery unit ("Battery D"). As he went to meet with his boisterous troops, Truman considered himself "the most thoroughly scared individual in that camp." When he ordered them to fall out, the men gave their new captain a Bronx cheer. The next day Truman busted most of his noncommissioned officers. "We knew that we had a different 'cat' to do business with than we had up to that time," one of his men later recalled. "He didn't hesitate at all."

## THE BATTLE OF WHO RUN

In the midst of their first battle, many Battery D members fled. Truman wasn't among them. He waved his arms, shouted, and called the remaining men every name he could think of. "The men think I am not much afraid of shells," he wrote Bess, "but they don't know I was too scared to run and that is pretty scared."

## PEDESTRIAN

Truman earned his men's devotion by giving his horse to injured soldiers and joining the rest on foot. When a colonel passing by ordered an infantryman with a sore ankle to dismount, Truman told him, "You can take these bars off my shoulders, but as long as I'm in charge of this battery the man's going to stay on that horse." The colonel rode off.

## PHILOSOPHY OF BUSINESS

After the war, Truman and fellow veteran Eddie Jacobson started a haberdashery in Kansas City. Despite some initial success, their venture failed. A clue as to why might be found in Truman's business philosophy. "When I buy a cow for $30 and then sell her to someone for $50," he once told Bess, "it always seems to me that I am really robbing that person of $20."

## POLITICIANS AND PROSTITUTES

At thirty-seven, the failed haberdasher turned to politics. Had he his druthers, Truman sometimes said, he'd have played piano for a living. Even as president, Truman often told male visitors (never the ladies), "My choice early in life was either to be a piano player in a whorehouse or a politician." After pausing for effect, he'd then add, "To tell the truth, there's hardly a difference."

## A FATE WORSE THAN DEATH

With the support of Kansas City's Pendergast machine, Truman ran to be an administrative "judge" of Jackson County. In his first speech as a candidate, Truman could barely stammer that he hoped those listening would vote for him. He later said of the experience, "I was scared worse than I was when I first came under fire in 1918."

## HUNG OVER

Truman pioneered the use of airplanes for campaigning when he hired a pilot to fly him over a picnic in Oak Grove, Missouri, in a rattletrap "Jenny." After they dropped a load of leaflets, Truman told the pilot to land near the picnickers so he could make a dramatic exit from the plane and address them. When the plane touched down, however, the pilot had trouble getting it to stop. It finally came to a halt barely three feet from a barbed-wire fence. Truman deplaned, strode to the fence, hung over it, and emptied the contents of his stomach. He then made his way to the rostrum and gave the crowd a talk.

### HOW TO DO BUSINESS

After being elected judge, Truman bought new seat covers for his car. The man from whom he bought them offered to install the covers for free if he'd send him some county work. "I don't do business that way," said Truman curtly as he paid his bill.

### A CONTRARY CUSS

When Jackson County voters passed a road-building bond issue, Judge Truman insisted that contracts go to low bidders. A group of road contractors who were used to getting road work as patronage protested to Tom Pendergast. Pendergast summoned Truman to his office to meet with them. The newly elected judge wouldn't budge on his sealed-bid policy. Pendergast threw up his hands. "Didn't I tell you boys," the Democratic boss said to the contractors, "he's the contrariest cuss in Missouri."

### ONE MAD MOM

A new road built while Truman was in office trimmed a piece off his mother's farm. He refused to have Jackson County compensate her. "I'd have gotten $11,000 if my boy wasn't county judge," she told a reporter. Martha Truman never stopped griping about her son's ethical fastidiousness in this instance.

## THE RIGHT STUFF

Although a partisan Democrat, Truman once supported a Republican named John Miles for county marshal. This later cost him votes when he was charged with being a disloyal Democrat. But Miles had been Truman's commanding officer in France. He'd seen him in places that made hell look like a playground, Truman told voters. He'd watched Miles and his men hold off a German attack when they were badly outnumbered. "He was of the right stuff," Truman concluded, "and a man who wouldn't vote for his comrade under circumstances such as these would be untrue to his country. I know that every soldier understands it. I have no apology to make for it."

## GREEN GROWS THE SENATOR

While running for the U.S. Senate in 1934, Truman suffered a sprained wrist and broken ribs during an auto accident. Nonetheless, he continued to speak and shake hands during a record succession of one-hundred-degree days. After he was elected and went to Washington, a reporter watched the grinning new senator introduce himself as "only a humble member of the next Senate, green as grass and ignorant as a fool about practically everything worth knowing." The reporter thought he was kidding. He soon came to realize, however, that this was just Harry Truman being himself.

## HOUSING

In a speech to the Kansas City Elks Club, Truman complained about Washington's rents. "Although it's hard to believe," he told the Elks, "there are some saphead senators who pay $1,500 a month for their apartments." An aide was able to find the Trumans (Harry, his mother-in-law, Bess, and their daughter, Margaret) a modest apartment for $100 a month. This aide then drove Senator Truman to a furniture store, where he bought some inexpensive pieces on time. After that the two went to a music store, where Harry tested every piano before renting one for $5 a month. Since he was now out of money, they made one last stop at the Hamilton National Bank so the senator could apply for a loan. Truman later told a group of bankers that he appreciated the way Hamilton's loan officer "was willing to float a little slow paper for me."

### FRESHMAN JITTERS

When he took up his work in the Senate, Truman said he felt "as timid as a country boy arriving on the campus of a great university for his first year." Unlike him, most of Truman's fellow senators were college graduates. Many had distinguished political pedigrees. Still, Truman never forgot the perspective offered by a more experienced colleague: "For the first six months you'll wonder how you got here. After that you'll wonder how the rest got here."

### A WORKHORSE

Truman discovered that most of the Senate's work was done by its least visible members. As a result, he set certain standards for his own tenure: Work hard, become expert on a few topics, devote more effort to committee work than speech-making. It would be some time before Truman rose to speak in the Senate. "I'm not going to demagogue until I have something to demagogue about," he explained.

## MOST POPULAR SENATOR

Bobby Baker was a Senate page during Truman's decade there. "Harry Truman was the most genteel man I ever met," Baker later recalled. "Not once did I see him act imperiously toward lowly page boys. 'Young man,' he would say—not 'Sonny,' as so many called us—'Young man, when it's convenient, could you please get me a glass of water?' Or, 'Young man, would you mind calling my secretary and asking her to send me such and so?' In any popularity contest among page boys of senators, I think Truman would have won in a landslide."

## A COMMON MAN

Truman's administrative aide Vic Messall told a pair of phone repairmen to help themselves to drinks from the icebox. Messall then left for an hour. When he returned, Truman's aide asked if anyone had stopped by. Only one man, the repairmen said. They'd asked the man if he wanted a drink. "We'll give you one but don't tell the senator we did," they told him, "because if the senator finds out we'll be fired." This man joined the two for a drink, then left. Messall asked what he looked like. Thick glasses, the phone men said. Medium height. Double-breasted suit. The man was Harry Truman.

## BEST QUALIFIED

Messall once brought Truman fifty folders of applications to West Point from boys in Missouri. Many were thick with recommendations from local panjandrums. The two went through each folder. One contained only a single piece of paper: a letter of application written in pencil on cheap paper. After reading the letter, Truman handed it to his aide. "Give him the appointment," he said.

SNOT-NOSED

A politician named Hugh Williamson once walked down a Kansas City street with Senator Truman. Both were dressed immaculately, with snow-white handkerchiefs in their breast pockets. A ragamuffin approached them. The boy was dirty, his clothes tattered. Mucus ran out of his nose and he kept tripping over an untied shoelace. Williamson made a wide detour around this boy. Truman went right up to him, knelt on one knee, took out his handkerchief, and blew the boy's nose. He then tied his shoelace, gave the boy some change, and sent him on his way with a friendly pat.

DOUBLE-TIME

Senator Truman was known for the brisk pace of his walk. The pace of a congressional aide named Richard Riedel was even brisker. To the delight of those watching, Truman one day fell in step behind Riedel and marched with him across the Capitol lobby like two double-timing soldiers.

NO HUNTING

Pennsylvania Senator Joseph Guffey invited Truman to join a hunting party at his game preserve. When gamekeepers herded animals in front of the hunters, however, Truman wouldn't shoot at them. "I do not like to hunt animals, and I never have," he once said. "I do not believe in shooting at anything that cannot shoot back."

NO SHAME

When Truman ran for reelection in 1940, the charge was made that his grandfather, Solomon Young, was a Jew. This would have made Truman himself at least partly Jewish. "I am not Jewish," he responded, "but if I were, I would not be ashamed of it."

## DOING THE RIGHT THING

Truman's opponent in the 1940 primary, Missouri Governor Lloyd Stark, berated Truman for his ties to the Pendergast machine. But Stark himself had run for governor with Pendergast support. Truman even had an old letter from his opponent thanking him for an introduction to Tom Pendergast. He never made this letter public. When a supporter asked why, Truman said, "I am not sure it would be the right thing to do."

## A STIFF OLD SENATOR

As war clouds gathered in 1940, Truman asked Army Chief of Staff George Marshall to activate him at his Reserve rank of colonel. The general pulled his glasses down on his nose and asked Missouri's senator how old he was. Fifty-six, said Truman. "We don't need old stiffs like you," Marshall told him. "You'd better stay home and work in the Senate." When Truman became Marshall's commander in chief, his appointments secretary asked the general what he'd say under those circumstances. "Well, I would tell him the same thing," said Marshall, "only I would be a little more diplomatic about it."

## THE TRUMAN COMMITTEE

Truman chaired a Special Committee to Investigate the National Defense Program. The "Truman Committee" saved billions of dollars and countless lives by exposing waste, fraud, and incompetence in the country's military complex. One of its most dramatic achievements was forcing the Navy to test its own tank carrier against one designed by shipbuilder Andrew Jackson Higgins. In a moderate sea, the Navy's craft foundered. Higgins's skimmed the waves, landed, unloaded its tank, put it back on board, then repeated this operation several times. His troop landing craft did just as well. Higgins's boats later landed at Normandy on D-Day.

## EQUAL TREATMENT

Following a driver who'd done the same thing, Truman went through a stoplight in Washington. A policeman pulled them both over. After examining Truman's license, the policeman asked if he was "the Truman Committee fellow." Truman said he was. "You've been doing a good job in there, Senator," said the policeman. "Just let me get this other fellow out of your road till I give him a ticket, then you can roll along."

"Officer," responded Truman, "I'm a citizen like anyone else. You give me a ticket." The policeman did so, reluctantly, but never sent him a summons. When he heard no more about the matter, Truman sent a contribution to the Policemen's Fund for the normal amount of a fine.

## A RELUCTANT CANDIDATE

Truman resisted strong pressure to become Franklin Roosevelt's running mate in 1944. Given Roosevelt's poor health, assuming he were reelected, the country's next vice president would most likely become its president. This had little appeal to Harry Truman. As he told Margaret, "1600 Pennsylvania is a nice address, but I'd rather not move in through the back door—or any other door at sixty."

## ON BOARD

When the Democrats convened in Chicago, FDR was in San Diego. Roosevelt took a call from Democratic National Committee Chairman Robert Hannegan. Truman stood beside Hannegan. The president's booming voice was easy to overhear. "Bob," he called out, "have you got that fellow lined up yet?"

"No," Hannegan replied. "He is the contrariest Missouri mule I've ever dealt with."

"Well," continued Roosevelt, "you tell him that if he wants to break up the Democratic Party in the middle of a war, that's his responsibility."

After Roosevelt hung up, Truman was subdued. Finally he murmured, "Well, if that is the situation, I'll have to say yes. But why in the hell didn't he tell me in the first place?"

## CHANGE OF ADDRESS

Before the 1944 campaign began, Truman and his army pal Eddie McKim visited the White House together. As they left, McKim said, "Hey, bud, turn around and take a look. You're going to be living in that house before long."

"Eddie, I'm afraid I am," replied Truman. "And it scares the hell out of me."

## FRIENDS

Less than a week after Truman became vice president, his friend and mentor Tom Pendergast died. Even though Pendergast had served time in prison for corruption, Truman attended his funeral in Kansas City. In response to the subsequent uproar, Truman said simply, "He was always my friend, and I have always been his."

## JUST WHISTLE

In a famous news photo, Lauren Bacall lounges with a come-hither look on top of a piano being played by Harry Truman. The vice president looks sheepishly over his shoulder. When asked what Bess said when she saw the picture, Truman replied, "She said she thought it was time for me to quit playing the piano."

## A FATEFUL MESSAGE

On April 12, 1945, Harry Truman had just finished presiding over a Senate session and was about to "strike a liquid blow for liberty" with House Speaker Sam Rayburn. As he mixed bourbon with branch water, Rayburn told Truman that White House Press Secretary Stephen Early wanted him to call. Truman did so. Early asked him to come right over. When Truman arrived, he was led to Eleanor Roosevelt's study. Mrs. Roosevelt put her hand on his shoulder. "Harry," she said, "the president is dead."

"Is there anything I can do?" stammered Truman.

"Is there anything *we* can do for *you?*" Mrs. Roosevelt responded. "For you are the one in trouble now."

## LEFTOVERS FOR DINNER

After taking the oath of office and meeting briefly with cabinet members, Truman returned to his apartment building. There he found his wife, daughter, and mother-in-law visiting a next-door neighbor. The new president ate a sandwich made from the neighbor's leftover turkey, then returned to their apartment, where he called his mother. After that, Truman wrote in his diary, "Went to bed, went to sleep, and did not worry any more."

## MORNING PRAYERS

At the White House, President Truman had his first meeting with reporters. "Boys, if you ever pray, pray for me now," he told them. "I don't know whether you fellows ever had a load of hay fall on you, but when they told me yesterday what had happened, I felt like the moon, the stars, and all the planets had fallen on me."

"Good luck, Mr. President," one reporter said.

"I wish you didn't have to call me that," responded Truman.

## COMMISERATION

After Franklin Roosevelt's funeral in Hyde Park, veteran White House correspondent Merriman Smith greeted Truman at the door of his train car. "I know you must be awfully sad," Truman told Smith with a sympathetic smile, "because you knew him so well." Struggling not to lose control, Smith murmured a thank you and turned to leave. The new president took Smith's arm and led him inside his train car. There he took a drink from a waiter and handed it to him. "Here, this may make you feel a little better," the president told the reporter.

## MATERNAL WISDOM

When asked how she felt about having a son in the White House, Martha Truman replied, "I can't really be glad he is president because I'm sorry that President Roosevelt is dead. If he had been voted in, I would be out waving a flag, but it doesn't seem right to be very happy or wave a flag now." Martha Truman's son Harry later said of his mother's statement, "If it had been prepared by the best public relations man it could not have been better."

## A HOUSE GUEST

Truman dispatched the presidential plane to bring his ninety-two-year-old mother to Washington. "Oh fiddlesticks," she commented when her son and a mob of journalists greeted her at the airport. "Why didn't you tell me there was going to be all this fuss, and I wouldn't have come."

Told she would be sleeping in Lincoln's room, the daughter of Confederates said she'd as soon sleep on the floor. After also passing on the overly ornate Rose Room, Martha Truman ended up in a maid's bedroom. To his pleasure and relief, Truman found that his mother "did not seem to feel that there was anything special about my being in the White House or my being president. She thought it was just the natural thing."

## ABSENTMINDED

The new president and his friend John Snyder were walking back to the White House from a meeting. As they reached the center of Pennsylvania Avenue, Truman suddenly stopped and exclaimed, "Oh, hell! I left my White House pass on the dresser."

## WALKING

As president, Truman continued his custom of taking early-morning walks for exercise. "Constitutionals," he called them. These walks usually took half an hour and covered up to two miles. At first, White House reporters thought the president's daybreak strolls were a public relations gimmick. After three weeks of getting up at six A.M. and trying to keep up with the fast-walking president, however, Merriman Smith concluded that this man *liked* getting up at dawn and taking a hike at a pace "normally reserved for track stars."

## FATHER-DAUGHTER COMMUNION

Truman once invited Margaret to join him on an early-morning walk. This would give them an opportunity to talk, he suggested. Within a block he had outdistanced his daughter by thirty feet. "Come on, Margie," the president called back. "What's holding you up?"

"Where's the fire?" she gasped.

Two blocks later Margaret Truman was sixty feet behind her father. "What's the matter with you, anyway?" he wondered.

"I'm wearing high heels," his daughter pointed out.

"Why don't you buy some sensible shoes?" asked her father.

This was the last time Margaret joined the president on his early-morning walk.

## SOUVENIRS

During his walks, Truman occasionally stopped for a cup of coffee. He always paid a dollar a cup. Some restaurateurs framed this dollar and put the cup itself on display. Did Truman realize what was up? At Washington's First Baptist Church, where the president sometimes worshiped, a five-dollar bill signed by him showed up in the collection basket. A note written on White House letterhead was attached to the bill. This note read, "The deacon who finds this bill can keep it as a souvenir if he puts two like it in its place."

## TIDDLYWINKS

White House staffers found the casual Trumans quite a change from the more reserved Roosevelts. During dinner one night, Harry flipped a watermelon seed at Bess, who returned the fire. Soon watermelon seeds were flying in every direction. A butler who braved the barrage as he tried to clear the table became a target of seeds as other servants stood by and howled.

LINCOLN SLEPT HERE

Truman asked usher J. B. West for a guided tour of the White House. In Lincoln's room, with its heavy Victorian furniture and huge bed, Truman asked if they'd dare evict Mr. Lincoln so his daughter could use it. West assured him that Lincoln probably slept in every room of the White House. He then reviewed how many times Truman's predecessors had moved furniture from one room to another, including the Lincoln Room. "Now I know why they say Lincoln's ghost walks around up here at night," Truman said with a chuckle. "He's just looking for his bed."

SELF-RELIANCE

When a torrential downpour hit Washington one night, the president got out of bed in his striped pajamas to see if rain was coming through the windows. It was. Truman gathered some bathroom towels and began to mop up the water. He did this for half an hour, until an usher heard the commotion and took over. On another occasion the president's valet found him washing his own socks and underwear. "I would have done more things for myself in the White House," he later wrote, "if the people around there had let me. The trouble was they were always grabbing bags and opening doors before I could get at them."

MAKING AMENDS

In the second month of his presidency, Truman heard that Herbert Hoover was in Washington. Bypassing the switchboard, he called Hoover at his hotel and asked if he could visit him there. Hoover said he'd come to the White House. "Well," responded Truman, "I took the liberty of anticipating you. I already have a car on the way over to your hotel to bring you." This was Herbert Hoover's first visit to his former home since Franklin Roosevelt defeated him in 1932. He was touched by the invitation and became a friend and sometime emissary for Truman. "When you came to the White House," Hoover later wrote his successor, "within a month you opened the door to me to the only profession I knew, public service, and you undid some disgraceful action that had been taken in the prior years. For all of this and your friendship I am deeply grateful."

## A REAL DRINK

Before addressing the founding conference of the United Nations in San Francisco, Truman hosted a diplomatic reception at his hotel. The only libation supplied by the State Department was a bowl of amber liquid they called "champagne punch."

"Hell, that stuff will rust your pipes," Truman observed to the foreign ministers and ambassadors surrounding him. "Come on up to my suite, gentlemen, and I'll pour you a real drink."

Their initial shock at Truman's words was replaced by broad grins among the diplomats, who dutifully followed him toward the elevators.

## UPSTAIRS ON THE FRONT PORCH

As he sailed to a summit conference in Potsdam, Germany, on the U.S.S. *Augusta,* Truman said he wanted to go up on the "front porch" for some fresh air. Reporters ribbed the president about using a landlubber's term for the forecastle deck, and for saying that he wanted to go upstairs and downstairs rather than above or below. "The only time I was ever at sea before was going to France and back in the last war," responded Truman. "Now, wouldn't it be silly for me to try to ape.the language of men whose business is ships?"

## AN OVERQUALIFIED PAGE-TURNER

When it was the United States's turn to supply an evening's entertainment at Potsdam, Truman summoned a twenty-seven year-old U.S. Army sergeant whom he'd heard was an accomplished pianist. The sergeant's name was Eugene List. The president asked List to play his favorite Chopin waltz: Opus 42. Before he performed, Truman warmed up the crowd with his own rendition of Paderewski's Minuet in G. List then took the bench and asked if someone could turn pages for him. To his astonishment, Truman himself volunteered. Throughout the performance, Truman stood beside the pianist turning pages of sheet music.

## NO FOOLING

At the end of one session at Potsdam, an Army public relations officer hitched a ride in Truman's limousine. As they drove, this soldier told the president that if there was anything he wanted—women, say—to let him know.

"Listen son, I married my sweetheart," responded a tight-lipped Truman. "She doesn't run around on me, and I don't run around on her. I want that understood. Don't ever mention that kind of stuff to me again."

## TOP SECRET

The first successful test of an atomic bomb took place in New Mexico during the Potsdam conference. A report of this test was sent to Truman. Shortly afterward, Truman took Stalin aside and told him that the United States had a super-bomb in production. The news didn't seem to surprise the Soviet leader. Stalin said simply that he was glad to hear about this weapon and hoped it would be put to good use against the Japanese. As it turned out, spies in the U.S. nuclear weapons program had been keeping the Soviets posted on its progress. "When I told Stalin about the atom bomb," Truman later recalled, "he merely shrugged his shoulders, as though he knew the secret all the time . . . which the son of a bitch probably did."

## TOUGH DECISION

Truman called his decision to drop atomic bombs on Japan "a purely military decision to end the war." In his own thinking and that of advisers, doing so was preferable to prolonging the conflict by invading Japan with untold casualties on both sides. Twenty years after Hiroshima and Nagasaki were leveled by atomic bombs, Truman elaborated on his thinking in a lecture: "It was a question of saving hundreds of thousands of American lives. I don't mind telling you that you don't feel normal when you have to plan hundreds of thousands of complete final deaths of American boys who are alive and joking and having fun while you are doing your planning. You break your heart and your head trying to figure out a way to save one life."

White House photographer Joe O'Donnell—who as a Marine photographer recorded the devastation in Hiroshima and Nagasaki—once asked the president if he had any misgivings about using such horrible weapons. "Hell yes!" Truman replied. "I've had a lot of misgivings . . . "

V-J DAY

After Japan surrendered, Truman walked along the inside perimeter of the White House fence shaking hands with thousands of deliriously happy Americans. He then called Eleanor Roosevelt to tell her, "I wished it had been President Roosevelt, and not I, who had given the message to our people."

WHAT REAL GENTLEMEN PREFER

White House usher J. B. West was better impressed with plain Bess Truman's unadorned look than with the tinted hair and heavy makeup favored by so many of Washington's society ladies. Asked about his wife's appearance, Truman himself said, "She looks exactly as a woman her age should look."

When a friend told Truman about the slogan he'd seen on a billboard—"Gentlemen Prefer Blondes"—the president responded: "Real gentlemen prefer gray."

I'LL CHRISTEN YOU

Although lively and witty in private, Bess Truman could seem dour and reserved in public. A plane-christening fiasco didn't help the first lady's image. Because no one had remembered to score the champagne bottle, it remained unscathed after nine whacks by Bess. Onlookers laughed. Margaret commented that this was a fine thing for a former girl shotput champion (which her mother actually was). A mechanic finally stepped forward to finish the job. When Truman saw newsreel footage of the episode, he told Bess it was amusing. She didn't agree. In fact, Bess reportedly told Harry, she was sorry he hadn't been there so she could swing the bottle at him.

## SOUNDS LIKE HIM

A reporter asked the president if he'd called a general a "squirrel head" as rumored. After saying he hadn't, Truman looked to Bess for confirmation. "Really?" observed his wife with an arched eyebrow. "It sounds just like you."

## NO MANURE

In one story that made the Washington rounds, a woman pleaded with Bess to clean up her husband's language. He'd recently called someone's comment "a bunch of horse manure." The First Lady was said to have smiled when she heard this and commented, "You don't know how many years it took to tone it down to that."

## TALK TO BESS

Nearly all presidents curse in private. Truman sometimes did so in public (leading Richard Nixon to say that we needed cleaner talkers in the White House). During an after-dinner speech to military officers the president complained that he was getting too much advice from journalists on whom to fire and hire. "No son of a bitch is going to dictate to me who I'm going to have!" said Truman. His expletive caused a stir. Later, a prominent clergyman commented that if similarly provoked he might have used the same language. When Truman heard this, he said, "I just wish that rector would go talk to my wife."

## TOO MANY FIREMEN

Truman made notes on his appointment sheet about what had transpired during meetings with visitors. Among them were:

(WILLIAM RANDOLPH HEARST, JR.) *Told me what papa thought. Explained, diplomatically, I didn't give a damn.*

(A GROUP OF EDUCATORS) *Gave me a song & dance on education.*

(DOROTHY AND DIANA ROOSEVELT) *Just came in. Don't know why.*

(CHESTER GRAY, FARMER'S ADVOCATE) *An old baloney peddler.*

Finally Truman sent Appointments Secretary Matthew Connelly a memo saying, "It seems to me that we have seen enough visiting firemen and potential promoters and chiselers." The volume of visitors went down.

## KICKED AROUND

Truman discussed the idea of creating a Missouri Valley Authority with Tennessee Valley Authority head David Lilienthal. Lilienthal said that he hoped an MVA would be as autonomous as the TVA. In such regional programs, he explained, people felt they could get at bureaucrats when necessary. Truman agreed. "Do you know why I go back home every once in a while?" he asked Lilienthal. "So people can kick me around."

## JUST CALL ME HARRY

During a trip to Missouri, President Truman attended the Pemiscot County Fair. There he discussed crop rotation with biboveralled farmers. When a mock steam locomotive rolled through the fairgrounds, Truman blew its whistle. He also played piano for some Methodist ladies. After one number he told them, "When I played this, Stalin signed the Potsdam agreement."

## OLD NOVOCAINE

Truman was furious when Soviet Ambassador Nicolai V. Novikov didn't attend the first White House state dinner of 1946. The next day he told Undersecretary of State Dean Acheson to have Novikov recalled. Acheson counseled restraint. Truman was adamant. The Soviet ambassador had insulted his wife, and he wanted nothing more to do with him. The phone on his desk rang. It was Bess. Bess asked to speak to Acheson. "You must not let Harry do what he's going to do," she said. After Mrs. Truman told him this, Acheson began to echo her supposed words: "above himself . . . delusions of grandeur . . . too big for his britches . . . "

Finally Truman grabbed the receiver, saying, "All right, all right. When you two gang up on me, I know I'm licked."

As Acheson left his office, Truman called out, "Tell Old Novocaine we didn't miss him!"

## HUSTLING WINNIE

As Harry Truman and Winston Churchill traveled by train to Fulton, Missouri, where Churchill was to give a speech, the Briton said he'd like to play some poker. Churchill thought he'd played something like it during the Boer War.

Before their game started, Churchill took his leave. While he was gone, Truman told his aides, "Men, we have an important task ahead of us. This man has been playing poker for more than forty years. He is cagey, he loves cards, and is probably an excellent player. The reputation of American poker is at stake, and I expect every man to do his duty."

Soon after the first hand was dealt, Churchill said to Truman, "Mr. President, I think that when we are playing poker I will call you Harry."

"All right, Winston," replied Truman.

The Americans soon realized that their English guest was not that good a poker player. After they'd played for an hour, Churchill again excused himself. Truman now changed the order of the day. Noting the Englishman's dwindling stack of chips, he told his gang that they weren't treating their guest very well.

"But, boss," responded military aide, Harry Vaughan, "*this guy's a pigeon!* If you want us to play our best poker for the nation's honor, we'll have this guy's pants before the evening is over. Now just tell us what you want. You want us to play customer poker, okay, we can carry him along all evening. If you want us to give it our best, we'll have his underwear."

Truman smiled. "I don't want him to think we are pushovers," he said, "but at the same time, let's not treat him badly."

After he returned, Churchill began to win some handsome pots. Charlie Ross even threw in a hand with one ace showing and another down against Churchill's visible jack. "Charlie studied what he knew had to be a winning hand," recalled Truman's assistant Clark Clifford, "looked over at the president, gave what I thought sounded like a sigh, and folded."

## BUZZING THE WHITE HOUSE

The DC-4 used to fly Truman about the country was formally called the "Flying White House." Informally the plane was dubbed the "Sacred Cow" because of its fat white silhouette. When the Sacred Cow left Washington for Independence in mid-1946, Truman noticed the swoops, dips, and dives of jet planes at an air show over National Airport. This gave him an idea. His wife and daughter were still in the White House. "Do you suppose," he asked pilot Hank Myers, "we could dive on them? Like a jet fighter? I've always wanted to try something like that."

"Well, there's no harm in it," Myers responded. "But somebody's sure gonna catch hell for it and I'm gonna blame you."

"I've got broad shoulders," said Truman. "How about it?"

The pilot changed course and flew directly over the White House. When Truman gave him the go-ahead, he quickly descended from three thousand to one thousand feet. At five hundred feet the pilot leveled off and roared past startled figures looking up at them from the White House roof. The second time they did this, Bess and Margaret were on the roof, jumping up and down and waving at the Sacred Cow. Although his wife and daughter couldn't see him, the president of the United States—his face pressed against a small window—waved and laughed back.

## FERTILIZING OHIO

Truman asked Myers to let him know every time they flew over Ohio. This was the home state of his political nemesis, Republican Senator Robert Taft. When told that Ohio was beneath them, Truman would saunter back to the lavatory. After he returned, the pilot emptied the plane's waste disposal system. Its contents evaporated and disintegrated before reaching the ground, of course, but to Truman it was the thought that counted.

### MOTHER KNOWS BEST

When Martha Truman broke a hip early in 1947, her son flew to his mother's bedside. Despite dire medical predictions, his mother rallied. Her renewed interest in politics was a good sign. She asked her boy if he was going to run for president the next year. Truman said he didn't know. "Don't you think it's about time you made up your mind?" she said.

Martha Truman died a few weeks later. "No one in the world can take the place of your mother," her son later wrote. "Right or wrong, from her viewpoint you are always right. She may scold you for little things, but never for the big ones."

### THINKING OF YOU

During a twilight walk, Truman decided to inspect the mechanism that raised and lowered part of the Memorial Bridge spanning the Potomac. There he encountered the man in charge of this operation. The bridge tender was eating his evening meal from a tin bucket. Not flustered in the least, he looked up at Truman and said, "You know, Mr. President, I was just thinking about you." Truman loved to tell others of this encounter.

### THE TRUMAN PLAN

In mid-1947 Truman and his aides developed a massive plan to rebuild Western Europe. Its official title was the European Recovery Program. This proposed program was announced in a commencement speech at Harvard by Secretary of State George Marshall. Clark

Clifford suggested that it be dubbed the Truman Plan. "Are you crazy?" responded the president. "If we sent it up to that Republican Congress with my name on it, they'd tear it apart. We're going to call it the Marshall Plan."

## DUPLICATE PLANS

Trainmen's union head Al Whitney had supported Truman for reelection to the Senate in 1940 when few others did. While resisting a railroad strike in 1946, however, President Truman called Whitney "an enemy of the people." In response Whitney said, "You can't make a president out of a ribbon clerk."

After Truman vetoed the antilabor Taft-Hartley Act in 1947, Whitney made an appointment to see him. Before entering the White House he walked around it twice, working up his nerve to go in. When Whitney finally entered the Oval Office, Truman greeted him with an outstretched hand. "It's good to see you Al," he said. "Let's not waste time discussing the past. Let's just agree we both received bad advice."

Whitney's eyes moistened. "Mr. President," he said, "I'm a third-generation Irishman who's part Scotch and you know they are kind of hotheaded sometimes."

"I'm made up on the same plan," responded Truman.

## CHIVALRY LIVES

Although he was less than avant-garde on women's rights, during his seven years as president Harry Truman appointed more women to positions requiring Senate approval than Franklin Roosevelt did in twelve. Truman also endorsed the concept of an Equal Rights Amendment. His rationale had a quaint flavor. "I have no fear of its effect on the home life of the American people," Truman said of the proposed constitutional amendment. "Nearly every man has his woman on a pedestal anyway and this will only make the legal aspects of the situation more satisfactory from the standpoint of the legal rights of the women of the country."

## FRIEND OF ISRAEL

Truman was under intense pressure to support or oppose a new state of Israel. When his Jewish friend Eddie Jacobson visited the White House, Truman made him promise not to raise the subject. Nonetheless, Jacobson tearfully pleaded with his Army pal to at least meet with Zionist leader Chaim Weizmann. As a clincher he pointed that Weizmann was as much a hero to him as Andrew Jackson was to Truman. "You win, you baldheaded son-of-a-bitch," Truman finally said. "I will see him."

At Truman's behest, the United States recognized the State of Israel eleven minutes after its proclamation in May 1948. "God put you in your mother's womb," Israel's chief rabbi later told Truman, "so you would be the instrument to bring about the rebirth of Israel after two thousand years." In response, tears rolled down the president's cheeks.

## RECONSTRUCTION

A group of civil rights leaders told Truman about shocking acts of violence against black veterans. In one case an Army sergeant had been beaten so savagely that he was left blind in one eye. After hearing of this incident, the president exclaimed, "My God! I had no idea it was as terrible as this. We've got to do something!"

In time he established a President's Committee on Civil Rights, initiated full integration of the armed forces, banned discrimination in federal hiring, introduced legislation to outlaw lynching, and revived the Fair Employment Practices Committee.

On the eve of 1948's Democratic convention, a delegation of southerners said they'd only support Truman for reelection if he'd soften his stand on civil rights. Truman wrote them:

> *My forebears were Confederates. I come from a part of the country where Jim Crowism is as prevalent as it is in New York or Washington. Every factor and influence in my background—and in my wife's for that matter—would foster the personal belief that you are right.*
>
> *But my very stomach turned over when I learned that Negro soldiers, just back from overseas, were being dumped out of army trucks in Mississippi and beaten.*
>
> *Whatever my inclinations as a native of Missouri might have been, as president I know this is bad. I shall fight to end evils like this.*

When South Carolina Governor Strom Thurmond subsequently ran for president as a "Dixiecrat," a reporter pointed out that Truman's support for equal rights was little different than Franklin Roosevelt's. "I agree," said Thurmond. "But Truman really means it."

## GIVING 'EM HELL

As Truman was about to embark on his quixotic 1948 campaign, running mate Alben Barkley said, "Go out there and mow 'em down." Truman responded, "I'll mow 'em down, Alben . . . and I'll give 'em hell." For the rest of the campaign, cries of "Give 'em hell,

Harry!" often emanated from crowds listening to Truman—sometimes shouted by his own aides.

### WHISTLE-STOPPING

Robert Taft accused the president of "blackguarding Congress at whistle-stops across the country." Truman pounced on this concept and rode it into the history books. During the 1948 campaign he traveled 31,700 miles by rail and gave 356 speeches, most of them from his train's rear platform. A set piece during many of these talks was the concluding moment when he asked, "How'd ja like to meet the family?" This usually met with a roar of assent. Bess would then walk through a curtain to join her husband on the train's rear platform. With a wink at the men in the audience he would introduce her as "The Boss." Then Margaret would join them to be introduced as "The Boss's boss." As their train pulled away, the Truman clan stood arm-in-arm, waving good-bye to the crowd shrinking before them.

### DRESSED FOR THE OCCASION

Truman's train arrived late one night in Missoula, Montana. A crowd of local residents had waited patiently for him to appear on its rear platform. And appear the president did, in bathrobe and pajamas. "I am sorry I had gone to bed," he told the crowd. "But I thought you would like to see what I look like, even if I didn't have on any clothes."

### HOW TO CATCH COLD

During a speech in Barstow, California, a woman called out, "President Truman, you sound as if you had a cold."

"That's because I ride around in the wind with my mouth open," Truman responded.

## OOMPAH

Truman liked to tell of campaigning on an Indian reservation. After each promise of what he'd do for Indians if elected, the crowd shouted, "Oompah! Oompah!" The louder this chorus grew, the more inspired Truman's speech became. As he left, the president had to cross a corral which had been filled with horses. "Careful," his Indian escort told him. "Don't step in the oompah."

## A SKEPTIC

Late in the campaign, *Newsweek* asked fifty political writers to predict its outcome. On October 12, Clark Clifford slipped off the campaign train to get *Newsweek*'s issue reporting the results. All fifty predicted a Dewey victory. As Clifford passed through the president's car on the way back to his own, with the magazine carefully hidden inside his coat, Truman said, "What does it say?"

"What does what say?" asked Clifford, feigning innocence.

"What have you got under your coat, Clark?"

"Nothing, Mr. President."

"Clark, I saw you get off the train just now and I think that you went in there to see if they had a newsstand with a copy of *Newsweek*. And I think maybe you have it under your coat."

Clifford handed it over. Truman glanced at the article in question, then gave it back to his aide. He seemed unruffled. "Don't worry about that poll, Clark," said the president. "I know every one of those fifty fellows, and not one of them has enough sense to pound sand into a rathole."

A GOOD NIGHT'S SLEEP

On election day, Truman relaxed with his family in Independence, predicted victory to reporters, then went to a nearby spa for a steam bath and turned in early. At four A.M., a Secret Service agent woke Truman and told him to turn on the radio. In his clipped accent, commentator H. V. Kaltenborn was saying that even though the president was well ahead of his challenger, he still didn't think Truman could win. During a speech some weeks later, Truman did an impromptu impersonation of Kaltenborn. After seeing this performance in a newsreel, the announcer wrote the president to compliment him on his "excellent imitation of one H. V. Kaltenborn making false predictions on election night." Kaltenborn added, "On inauguration day I told my radio audience how much we should all appreciate the generous and genial spirit with which you dealt with those who were dumbfounded by your victory. It showed, I said, that for the next four years we can all be human with Truman, as well as grateful for a leader with a sense of humor. Millions of Americans like you better as they have come to know you better."

AN HONEST MAN

After Truman's stunning upset, his friend George Allen confessed, "I was supremely confident of your defeat."

"So was everybody else," responded Truman, with a jab to Allen's ribs. "But you're the first one who's admitted it."

CROW *EN GLÂCE*

Following the election, staff members of the Washington *Post* invited Truman to a "Crow Banquet." At this affair, all reporters, commentators, columnists, and pollsters were to be fed crow *en glâce.*

The president would eat turkey. He would wear white tie, they sackcloth. Truman responded that he had "no desire to crow over anybody or to see anybody eat crow figuratively or otherwise. We should all get together now and make a country in which everybody can eat turkey whenever he pleases."

### RSVP

In response to his own invitation to inaugural festivities, Truman wrote, "Weather permitting, I hope to be present."

### INSOLENCE

During a poker game at Clark Clifford's home, Chief Justice Fred Vinson needed only a jack or lower to win a large pot. Truman was dealing. "Okay, Mr. President, hit me," said Vinson. Truman dealt him a queen of spades. "You son of a bitch!" exclaimed Vinson. A hush ensued. Finally Vinson stammered, "Oh, Mr. President, Mr. President . . . " With that the group laughed so hard that they woke up Clifford's sleeping mother. Truman laughed harder than anyone. Retelling this story became a favorite pastime of the president and his pals. During a subsequent gathering, they held a mock trial of Vinson. The chief justice pleaded that his exclamation was "ejaculatory only and not addressed to the president." Truman's verdict: "not proven."

### STUDIES IN PROBABILITY

Although much was made of the president's propensity for poker ("a study in probability," he called the game), Truman usually played for low stakes and was not that good a player. For one thing, he was cautious, sometimes driving fellow players to distraction as he studied his hand. Another problem was Truman's lack of killer instinct. "He never wanted to beat anyone," said former aide Vic Messall. "I saw him turn down four aces one night so someone who wasn't doing well could win a pot."

## CARD SHARP

Among those who sometimes played poker on the presidential yacht, the *Williamsburg,* was a young congressman named Lyndon Johnson. Like Truman, Johnson seemed to enjoy the banter more than the game itself. Clark Clifford watched the future president soak up political lore during these sessions. "Although I did not realize it at the time," he later wrote, "the *Williamsburg* poker games and the inevitable political discussions were part of a continuing seminar on the study of power."

## LOBBYING

One poker pal of Truman's was a former Senate colleague turned lobbyist. Every few months he'd drop by the Oval Office to chat with the president. As he left, the ex-senator would say, "Oh, by the way, Mr. President, I promised a friend of mine I'd mention case so and so to you."

"Fine, fine," Truman would respond, "you mentioned it. Good day."

After one such exchange, Truman said to his aide John Steelman, "He probably got five or ten for that, but you better watch it, John, there must be something wrong with it or they wouldn't have hired him to see me."

## TABLOID JUSTICE

Truman met with advisers to consider ways to counter McCarthyism. One aide mentioned that a dossier had been compiled detailing Joseph McCarthy's illicit liaisons with women. Publicizing this information would cook the Wisconsin senator's goose. Truman slapped the table hard, saying he wanted no more such talk. Writer John Hersey, who attended this meeting, was struck in particular by three comments that Truman made to explain his position:

*You must not ask the president of the United States to get down in the gutter with a guttersnipe.*

*Nobody, not even the president of the United States, can approach too close to a skunk, in skunk territory, and expect to get anything out of it except a bad smell.*

*If you think somebody is telling a big lie about you, the only way to answer is with the whole truth.*

## FRIENDSHIP

When Alger Hiss was accused of being a communist spy, Secretary of State Dean Acheson said he would not turn his back on his law partner and former aide. During the ensuing uproar, Acheson offered to resign. Truman wouldn't let him. The president told Acheson that he understood why he'd taken such a stand. Truman said he knew about friendship, and mentioned the controversy when he attended Tom Pendergast's funeral. "God damn it, Dean," Truman concluded, "if you think a man who followed an old criminal to his grave because he was his friend would have you do anything different than you did, you don't know me."

## LOYALTY

One of Truman's greatest strengths—and most glaring weaknesses—was his devotion to friends. From Army buddies through the Pendergasts to Dean Acheson and George Marshall, Harry Truman stood by those he thought had earned his loyalty. When this loyalty was abused by petty corruption among friends in his administration, Truman paid a stiff political price. It was a price he was willing to pay. In the midst of Truman's second term, journalist William Hillman told him, "You know, it is said about you that you have stood by a man to the last drop of mercy."

"I would rather have that said about me than to be a great man," responded the president.

## BLOWING SMOKE

Even though he considered Douglas MacArthur an unpredictable prima donna, Truman put him in charge of UN forces sent to help defend South Korea from invasion by North Korea. MacArthur proved to be a difficult field commander, prone to follow his own head rather than obey orders from Washington. In October 1950, Truman met with the general on Wake Island. During their first meeting, MacArthur asked the president if he minded him smoking his pipe. "No," replied Truman. "I suppose I have had more smoke blown at me than any other man alive."

## OUTPLACEMENT

When MacArthur's insubordination continued, Truman relieved him of his duties. A young White House staffer advised the president to say that this decision had been made with the unanimous backing of his advisers. "Son," responded Truman, "not tonight.

Tonight I am taking this decision on my own responsibility as president of the United States and I want nobody to think I am sharing it. Tonight it is my decision and mine alone."

After announcing his most controversial act as president, Truman went home and got a good night's sleep. When a reporter later observed that sacking MacArthur took guts, he responded, "Courage didn't have anything to do with it. General MacArthur was insubordinate and I fired him. That's all there was to it."

### A GOOD HOST

Late one afternoon, naval aide Robert Dennison was briefing Truman on an important matter regarding Korea. Matt Connelly interrupted them to ask if the president could see four visitors from Iowa. Truman said he could. Although he had no jurisdiction in the problem that concerned them—a local road and bridge issue—Truman listened patiently and made some suggestions. The group left looking elated. After they'd gone, Dennison said he couldn't understand why, with so many important matters before him, the president would take time to discuss a matter on which he could offer no actual help. "Sure it's not a problem I can solve," Truman responded. "It isn't a national problem, and maybe to you it isn't a problem, but believe me, to these people it's a problem. I'm the president of the United States and I should listen to people like that who are in trouble, even if that's all I can do."

### A NEMESIS IN NEED

A Missouri journalist wrote a front-page editorial lambasting the president for ignoring his home state. A few months later this journalist dropped from sight. Friends heard he was in financial straits.

What had happened to him? a mutual friend asked Truman. The president said he'd heard the man was working in Kansas City. At a newspaper job? No, said Truman, he was out of the writing business. Had the president heard from him recently? Fairly recently, said Truman. How recently was that? A couple of weeks ago. Did he know where the man was working? Yes, he did. And where was that? Oh, said Truman, he had a little job with the county. Did the president get him that job?

"No," responded an embarrassed Truman. "All I did was recommend him for it."

LOVEBIRDS

When Margaret went away to college, Harry and Bess spent a lot of time alone. Their staff began to call them "the lovebirds." After Bess spent a summer in Independence with her mother, Truman was jubilant when she returned. The next morning, Bess consulted with head butler J. B. West. They had a problem with the president's bed, she said. Could he get it fixed?

"Why certainly," replied West. "What's the matter?"

"Two of the slats broke down during the night," replied the first lady.

A TOUGH DAY AT THE OFFICE

When the White House needed extensive renovation, the Trumans moved across the street to Blair House. On the afternoon of November 1, 1950, Harry was napping there. At 2:20, two Puerto Rican nationalists stormed the house with guns blazing. They were able to get off twenty-seven shots before one was killed and the other wounded by guards. One guard died and two others were wounded in the exchange. Truman watched this episode from an upstairs window. He kept a speaking date later that day, seemingly none the worse for wear. "I never saw a calmer man," said Charlie Ross. "A president has to expect these things," Truman explained. "The only thing you have to worry about is bad luck. I never had bad luck." Several years after his presidency ended, Truman protested vehemently when he learned that a brass plaque honoring the guard who died defending him had been moved from outside Blair House.

## NERVES

After graduating from college, Margaret Truman became a professional concert singer. When she sang in Washington's Constitution Hall in 1949, her father sat in the president's box, dabbing his eyes and mangling two programs. "Don't be upset if I start tearing up my programs during the concert," he'd warned Margaret's voice coach, who sat beside him. "I always do that when I'm nervous."

## THE LOSS OF A FRIEND

On December 5, 1950, Charlie Ross died of a heart attack. Truman's handwritten eulogy to his press secretary began, "The friend of my youth, who became a tower of strength when the responsibilities of high office so unexpectedly fell to me, is gone." Truman took this statement down the hall and started reading it to reporters. But his voice cracked and he couldn't continue. "Ah, hell," the president finally said. "I can't read this thing. You fellows know how I feel anyway. . . ." With tears streaming down his face, he handed them his statement and walked back to his office.

A MAD DAD

A few hours after Ross died, Margaret Truman sang again in Constitution Hall. "Miss Truman cannot sing very well," reported Washington *Post* music critic Paul Hume. "She is flat a good deal of the time. . . . There were few moments during Margaret Truman's recital when one can relax and feel confident that she will make her goal, which is the end of the song."

After reading this review, her father exploded. "I have just read your lousy review of Margaret's concert," Truman wrote Hume in a longhand note. "I've come to the conclusion that you are 'an eight ulcer man on four ulcer pay.' It seems to me that you are a frustrated old man who wishes he could have been successful. When you write such poppycock . . . it shows conclusively that you're off the beam and at least four of your ulcers are at work. Someday I hope to meet you. When that happens you'll need a new nose, a lot of beefsteak for black eyes, and perhaps a supporter below."

When it was made public, Truman's letter provoked a national uproar. The president was denounced for his vulgarity. Few took into account the fact that Charles Ross had just died, and that things were going badly in Korea. Paul Hume himself commented, "I can only say that a man suffering the loss of a friend and carrying the burden of the present world crisis ought to be indulged in an occasional outburst of temper."

SOMETHING IN COMMON

When Joseph Short was sworn in as Charlie Ross's successor, his nine-year-old son Steve didn't want to attend because he was missing two front teeth. His parents made him go. Soon after the Short family was escorted into the president's office, Steve and the president disappeared. A few moments later both emerged from behind a set of curtains and the ceremony commenced. On the way home, Steve's mother asked him what he and the president had been up to. "You know, Mother," he said, "now I don't mind not having those two front teeth out. The president took me behind the curtain to show me that he had a tooth out, and the only difference is, he is going to have his capped today and I have to wait until mine grows in."

### SECOND THOUGHTS

When no promising Democrat stepped forward to run for president in 1952, Truman reconsidered his own decision not to stand for reelection. "Matt," he asked his appointments secretary one day, "do you think the old man will have to run again?"

"Would you do that to her?" responded Connelly, pointing to Bess Truman's picture.

Truman pondered Connelly's response. "You know," he finally said, "if anything happened to her, what would happen to me?"

"All right," said Connelly. "I think you've thought about it."

### A TOUGH MOVE

After seven years as president, Truman found packing his papers and belongings an imposing task. In the midst of this chore, West Virginia Senator Harley Kilgore visited Truman in the White House. "If I had known there would be so much work leaving this place," the president told him, "I'd have run again."

### A DISLIKED IKE

Truman's interaction with Dwight Eisenhower during the inauguration was less than cordial. First Eisenhower turned down an invitation to lunch with the outgoing president. Ike then refused to follow tradition and enter the White House to greet his predecessor. Not wanting to delay the ceremony, Truman came out and joined Eisenhower in his car. During their ride to the capital, Ike said he hadn't attended Truman's inauguration four years earlier because he didn't want to draw attention away from the president. "You were not here because I didn't send for you," snapped Truman. "But if I *had* sent for you, you would have come."

After the two got out of their car at the Capitol and waited to walk up to the platform, Eisenhower said, "I wonder who is responsible for my son John being ordered to Washington from Korea? I wonder who is trying to embarrass me?"

In fact, Truman himself had summoned Major John Eisenhower from Korea, where he was not serving in any vital capacity. "The president of the United States ordered your son to attend the inauguration," Truman told Eisenhower. "If you think somebody was trying to embarrass you by this order, then the president assumes full responsibility."

Eisenhower later thanked Truman for this thoughtful gesture, and for not letting him know about it in advance.

GET A GRIP

On his first morning home, the ex-president took a walk. A reporter asked him what the first thing was he planned to do that day. Responded Truman: "Carry the grips up to the attic."

UNEMPLOYED

Truman and his family returned to Independence. When their neighbors welcomed them back, Harry said, "After I get finished with the job Mrs. Truman has for me—unpacking—I'll be open for dinner engagements. I may be hungry. I don't have a job."

### LAWN CARE

If Harry could take walks, Bess observed, he could mow the lawn. Their grass grew longer and longer. Finally, one Sunday morning, Truman took out the mower and started mowing. Neighbors going to and from church got a clear picture of what the former president was doing instead of attending service. When Bess emerged from the house on her own way to church, she asked Harry, "What do you think you are doing?"

"I'm doing what you asked me to do," replied her smiling husband.

The next day Bess hired a lawn man.

### HARD FEELINGS

During a visit to Washington a few months after he left office, Truman was studiously ignored by his successor. When a reporter asked why he wasn't meeting with President Eisenhower, Truman replied, "He hasn't time to see every Tom, Dick, and Harry that comes to town."

### WHERE WERE YOU WHEN I NEEDED YOU?

The ex-president was offered a wide range of lucrative, undemanding positions in private industry. According to Truman, one television network wanted to pay him $50,000 to do some political commentary. Mike Todd offered "a fabulous salary" to head a merger he was organizing. Several oil companies pursued the ex-president, and an insurance company offered him $100,000 to chair its board.

He turned them all down. To explain why, Truman referred to his years as a struggling farmer. "It was a bad time for farmers," he said, "and I had to work mighty hard to make a go of it. If you had come around then and offered me this job, I'd have been glad to talk business with you."

Truman added, "Of course, they didn't want me; they wanted the presidency."

## NO MOOCHING

Truman thanked a man for sending two hundred color prints of a picture of him. Accompanying his letter was a check for $200. "I have been trying my level best," explained the ex-president, "as the people, in the time of Mark Twain, would say out West, not to be in a position of asking favors for no good reason, except the reason that I was in the White House. . . . If there is anything in the world that I dislike, it is a man who is always mooching things, based on some service he may have rendered publicly."

## BIG SPENDER

Truman launched a fund drive for his presidential library in Independence. One little girl donated fifty cents in dimes. Truman sent her a certificate awarded only to big donors. "This fifty cents to her is probably more than $5,000 by comparison," he explained.

## A STRIKING RESEMBLANCE

San Francisco shipping magnate George Killion invited the former president to dinner. When his driver got lost, Truman rang the doorbell of a nearby house to ask for directions. The man who answered said he couldn't help him. "I hope I'm not hurting your feelings," he added, "but you look exactly like that old s.o.b. Harry Truman."

"I hope I'm not hurting your feelings either," responded Truman, "but I *am* that s.o.b."

## A YANK AT OXFORD

Four years after he left office, Truman was awarded an honorary degree from Oxford. His *Doctoris in Iure Civili* (Doctor of Civil Law) degree referred to its recipient as "Harricum Truman." Oxford's public orator said, "The seers saw not your defeat, poor souls! Vain prayers, vain promises, vain Gallup Poll!" As Truman departed, Oxford students called out "Give 'em hell, Harricum!"

"Never, never in my life," he told a reporter covering the event, "did I ever think I'd be a Yank at Oxford."

## NO HARD FEELINGS

In 1958, Paul Hume—the Washington *Post* music critic whom Truman had lambasted eight years earlier—visited the Truman Library. While there, he asked to see the ex-president. Truman laughed when his guest's name was announced. He came out, gave Hume a tour of the library, then spent an hour visiting with his ex-nemesis. "I've had a lot of fun with you and General MacArthur over the years," Truman told Hume. "I hope you don't mind."

## SENSITIVITY

Truman reviewed his years as president with commentator Eric Sevareid. During their conversation, an aide of Truman's observed that one member of his Cabinet should probably have been fired. "No, no," said Truman. "That would not have been right. There were other ways to do it. What you don't understand is the power of a president to hurt." Truman explained that a word, a glance, or a thoughtless gesture by the nation's chief executive could scar someone for life. As opposed to his awesome power to set events in motion, Sevareid later wrote, the power of a president to hurt feelings was not something he'd ever considered. He added, "And still less had it occurred to me that a president in office would have the time and the need to be aware of this particular power among so many others."

EMPATHY

A decade after he left the White House, Truman lectured at a California college. Following his talk, a student rose to ask, "Mr. President, what do you think of our local yokel [then-Governor Pat Brown]?" Truman chastised the boy for being so disrespectful of his state's governor. Fighting tears, the student sat down. Afterward, Truman sought him out to shake hands and explain that his comment referred to the principle involved, and not to take it personally. Truman later asked the college's dean to keep him posted on this student's progress. The dean did so. Truman also corresponded with the boy. "I realized after I spoke that way," he told Margaret, "that I had unintentionally humiliated that young man. I was afraid that the memory of my harsh tone might scar his whole life and ruin his reputation among his friends and acquaintances."

STILL READING

During a business trip to New York, Truman was visited in his hotel room by an editor from Doubleday. The former president was sitting in a chair beside a table stacked with books. Did he like to read himself to sleep at night? the editor asked. "No, young man," replied Truman. "I like to read myself awake."

## NO PROBLEM

When in New York, Truman usually stayed at the Carlyle. This hotel's elevator once got stuck with him inside. After being freed, Truman assured the Carlyle's manager that he wasn't upset. In fact, said the ex-president, he'd enjoyed "a very pleasant few minutes talking to the people on the second floor through that part of the elevator door which could be opened."

## SHAVE AND A HAIRCUT

When Fidel Castro came to this country for a United Nations session in 1960, Truman thought Eisenhower missed a great opportunity by not meeting with the Cuban dictator. If he were still president, said Truman, "I'd've given him a big reception. I'd've had our picture taken together, then said to him, 'Fidel, you're a nice boy, and so far you've done a pretty good job. Now go back to Havana, shave, change those dirty clothes, and leave everything else to me.'"

## PRIORITIES

A television crew needed to reshoot parts of an interview with Truman about his decision to intervene in Korea. The former president inadvertently wore a necktie different from the one he'd had on originally. When the producer pointed this out, Truman gave him a withering look. "Does it *really* matter?" he asked. "Because if while I'm talking about Korea people are asking each other about my necktie, it seems to me we're in a great deal of trouble."

NO FRIEND FORGOTTEN

In February 1966, a man Truman knew was about to be buried in an Independence cemetery. Only the undertaker and a minister stood by his casket. At the burial time announced in the newspaper, a green Chrysler drew up. Harry Truman emerged. Even though he was eighty-three by then, in poor health, and the weather was bitterly cold, Truman stood by the bier throughout the ceremony. Later, the minister asked Truman why he'd subjected himself to such an ordeal. "Pastor," he said, "I never forget a friend."

CLOSE TO HOME

Truman was briefed on plans for his own funeral. He said the ceremony sounded like "a damn fine show," and was sorry he'd have to miss it. His only objection was to lying in state in Washington. Truman preferred to stay in his library's courtyard, where he wanted to be buried. "I like the idea because I may just want to get up someday and stroll into my office," he told Bess. "And I can hear you saying, 'Harry—you oughtn't!'"

UP IN SMOKE

One Christmas, Harry discovered Bess burning letters he had written her.

"You shouldn't be doing that!" he exclaimed.

"Why not?" she said. "I've read them several times."

"But think of history," pleaded Harry.

"I have," replied Bess.

Luckily, enough of Truman's letters survived to illustrate his writing at its best.

# *Love, Harry*

*Just as Dad did not really change when he became president, his letters from that period were as forthright and affectionate as his earlier ones. One generally has to look to the date of the letter rather than to its tone or content to recognize that this momentous change in his life had taken place.*

—MARGARET TRUMAN

❦

*April 21, 1945*

Dear Mamma and Mary:

Well, I've been the president for nine days. And such nine days no one ever went through before I don't believe. The job started at 5:30 in the afternoon of the 12th. It was necessary for me to begin making decisions an hour and a half before I was sworn in and I've been making them ever since. . . .

---

NOTE: Letters addressed to "Margie" are to Truman's daughter Margaret; to "Mamma" are to his mother Martha; to "Mamma and Mary" are to his mother and sister Mary Jane; to "Mary" or "Mary Jane" are to his sister alone; to "Ethel," "Nellie," or both are to his cousins Ethel and Nellie Noland.

May 13, 1945

Dear Mrs. [Emmy] Southern [an in-law of Bess's]:

... It is a peculiar American complex to want to know what their president eats, how he sleeps, when he gets up, what meats he prefers, etc. ad lib. I told 'em I was very fond of Elk and Buffalo meat. I didn't elaborate on it by telling them I'd had some fine pork tenderloin in Buffalo, N.Y. and a tip-top steak in Elk Springs, Wyoming.

They want to know my favorite songs and when I say "Pilgrims Chorus" from Parsifal or "Toreador" from Carmen or "Hinky Dinky Parlez Vous" or "Dirty Gerty from Bizerte," they are not sure whether I'm on the beam or not. . . .

June 12, 1945

Dear Bess:

Just two months ago today, I was a reasonably happy and contented vice president. Maybe you can remember that far back too. But things have changed so much it hardly seems real.

I sit here in this old house and work on foreign affairs, read reports, and work on speeches—all the while listening to the ghosts walk up and down the hallway and even right in here in the study. The floors pop and the drapes move back and forth—I can just imagine old Andy and Teddy having an argument over Franklin. Or James Buchanan and Franklin Pierce deciding which was the more useless to the country. And when Millard Fillmore and Chester Arthur join in for place and show the din is almost unbearable. But I still get some work done. . . .

❦

*July 3, 1945*

Dear Mamma and Mary:

. . . I am getting ready to go see Stalin and Churchill and it is a chore. I have to take my tuxedo, tails, Negro preacher coat, high hat, low hat and hard hat as well as sundry other things. I have a brief case filled up with information on past conferences and suggestions on what I'm to do and say. Wish I didn't have to go but I do and it can't be stopped now. . . .

❦

*July 18, 1945*
*Potsdam*

Dear Mamma:

. . . Mr. Stalin made a motion at the conference that I act as chairman and Churchill seconded it. So I preside. It is hard as presiding over the Senate. Churchill talks all the time and Stalin just grunts but you know what he means. . . .

❦

*August 12, 1945*

Dear Mamma:

. . . Since I wrote you last Tuesday there hasn't been a minute. The speech, the Russian entry into the war, the Japs' surrender offer and the usual business of the president's office have kept me busy night and day. It seems that things are going all right. Nearly every crisis seems to be the worst one but after it's over it isn't so bad. . . .

❧

*September 22, 1945*

Dear Mamma and Mary:

. . . I have almost as many prima donnas around me as Roosevelt had but they are still new at it. They don't get humored as much by me as they did by him. I fire one occasionally and it has a salutary effect. . . .

❧

*December 28, 1945*
*not sent*

Dear Bess:

Well I'm here in the White House, the great white sepulcher of ambitions and reputations. I feel like a last year's bird's nest which is on its second year. Not very often I admit I am not in shape. I think maybe that exasperates you too, as a lot of other things I do and pretend to do exasperate you. But it isn't intended for that purpose. . . .

You can never appreciate what it means to come home as I did the other evening after doing at least 100 things I didn't want to do and have the only person in the world whose approval and good opinion I value look at me like I'm something the cat dragged in and tell me I've come in at last because I couldn't find any reason to stay away. I wonder why we are made so that what we really think and feel we cover up?. . .

Kiss my baby and I love you in season & out.

*February 25, 1946*

Dear Mr. [William] Southern:

Bess called my attention to an article in the Independence Examiner Saturday, February sixteenth edition, in which a proposal is made to change the name of Van Horn Road to Truman Road.

If you will remember when I was Presiding Judge of the County Court, people wanted to name every road in the county for me and I wouldn't allow it. The only place my name appears is on the new Court House in Kansas City and the remodeled one in Independence, along with other members of the court and the architects, in very inconspicuous places. I have no desire to have roads, bridges, or buildings named after me. . . .

*June 12, 1946*

Dear Margie:

. . . They are fixing the hole in the middle of the hallway, opposite my study door. All the rugs are rolled back and a great scaffold has been constructed under the hole. Looks like they intend to hang a murderer in the White House hallway. There are some gentlemen in Congress—and out of it—who would take great pleasure in hoisting your dad on that scaffold! But they'll have to catch him first. I hope to dry some of their political hides on a frame before I'm through. I'm giving 'em both barrels of the blunderbuss from here out.

August 9, 1946

Dear Bess:

*Two* letters today! Made it very bright and happy. You know that there is no busier person than your old man—but he's never too busy or too rushed to let his lady love, the only one he ever had, hear from him every day no matter what portends. . . .

August 23, 1946

My dear Daughter:

. . . I am glad you are working hard at your music. If you love it enough to give it all you have, nothing can stop you. There is only one thing I ask—please don't become a temperamental case. It is hard to keep from it. I know—and no one knows better than I. But it is not necessary nor does it help your public relations. It makes no friends and to succeed at anything you must have friends on whom you can rely. . . .

February 19, 1947

Dear Mamma and Mary:

. . . Last night was our last reception and thank goodness. It was the Congressional. There were 760 paws to shake, which was fewer than usual. Most of the Senators and Congressmen I was glad to see, but there were half [a] dozen I'd rather have punched in the nose. I told Bess if she'd trip [Senator John] Bricker up so he'd sprawl on the floor in front of us I'd give her the big diamond out of the scimitar the Crown Prince of Arabia gave me. . . .

❧

*September 28, 1947*

Dear Bess:

. . . Believe it or not, I went to church this morning! Had a hundred thousand words to read for tomorrow's conference with the congressional leaders and the reorganization commission—so decided to let the words go to hell and I'd go to church.

❧

*November 14, 1947*

Dear Mary:

. . . The people can never understand why the president does not use his supposedly great power to make 'em behave. Well all the president is, is a glorified public relations man who spends his time flattering, kissing, and kicking people to get them to do what they are supposed to do anyway.

Then the family have to suffer too. No one of the name dares do what he'd ordinarily be at liberty to do because of the gossips. They say I'm my daughter's greatest handicap! Isn't that something? Oh well take care of yourself and some day the nightmare will be over and maybe we can all go back to normal living. . . .

❧

*December 3, 1947*

My dear Daughter:

. . . You should call your mamma and dad *every time* you arrive in a town . . . Some day maybe you'll understand what torture it is to be worried about the only person in the world that counts. You should know by now that your dad has only three such persons. Your ma, you, and your Aunt Mary. And your Aunt Mary is running around just as you are. So—you see besides all the world and the United States I have a couple of other worries. . . .

*June 28, 1948*

Dear Bess:

Twenty-nine years! It seems like twenty-nine days. . . .

You are still on the pedestal where I placed you that day in Sunday School in 1890. What an old fool I am.

*August 18, 1948*

Dear Ernie {Ernest W. Roberts, friend who urged caution on civil rights]:

. . . I am going to send you a copy of the report of my Commission on Civil Rights and then if you still have that antebellum proslavery outlook, I'll be thoroughly disappointed in you.

The main difficulty with the South is that they are living eighty years behind the times and the sooner they come out of it the better it will be for the country and themselves. I am not asking for social equality, because no such thing exists, but I am asking for equality of opportunity for all human beings and, as long as I stay here, I am going to continue that fight. When the mob gangs can take four people out and shoot them in the back, and everybody in the country is acquainted with who did the shooting and nothing is done about it, that country is in a pretty bad fix from a law enforcement standpoint.

When a mayor and a city marshal can take a Negro sergeant off a bus in South Carolina, beat him up and put out one of his eyes, and nothing is done about it by the state authorities, something is radically wrong with the system.

On the Louisiana and Arkansas Railway when coal burning locomotives were used, the Negro firemen were the thing because it was a backbreaking job and a dirty one. As soon as they turned to oil as a fuel it became customary for people to take shots at the Negro firemen and a number were murdered because it was thought that this was now a white-collar job and should go to a white man. I can't approve of such goings on and I shall never approve it, as long as I am here, as I told you before, I am going to try to remedy it and if that ends up in my failure to be reelected, that failure will be in a good cause. . . .

❧

*October 5, 1948*

Dear Mary:

. . . The trip just ended was a most strenuous one. I started out with a sore throat and the dust at Dexter, Iowa, just west of Des Moines, didn't help it any. Dr. Graham just sprayed, mopped, and caused me to gargle bad tasting liquids until the throat gave up and got well. . . .

We had tremendous crowds everywhere. From 6:30 in the morning until midnight the turnout was phenomenal. The news jerks didn't know what to make of it—so they just lied about it!. . .

September 8, 1949

Dear Nellie and Ethel:

. . . I'll tell you a secret which you must not under any circumstances repeat. Coming from Des Moines Tuesday, No. 4 engine on my fine plane conked out! You should have seen the scurrying and running to & fro. I sat still and watched 'em. Then we straightened out and came in on 3 engines. We were only up 6000 feet so there was no jump out and anyway I wouldn't jump until everybody else had—and it couldn't have been done at 6000. What a headline that would have made! I ordered no report—and there wasn't any. . . .

*October 29, 1949*

Dear Nellie:

. . . Margie has had a grand reception. The press has been kind and so have the critics. She sent me a paper from Winston-Salem, N.C. and wrote on the front of it—"Dear Daddy: I hope you'll notice my picture on page one—you'll find yours on page 18." Can you beat that?. . .

*November 28, 1949*

Dear Dean [Acheson]:

It was good of you to see us off. You always do the right thing. I'm still a farm boy and when the Secretary of State of the greatest Republic comes to the airport to see me off on a vacation, I can't help but swell up a little.

*September 24, 1950*

Dear Ethel:

. . . You know I have a valet, four ushers, five butlers, seven or eight secretaries, a dozen or so executive assistants, an assistant president—three of 'em in fact—and I can't open a door, get my hat, pull out my chair at the table, hang up my coat, or do anything else for myself—even take a bath! I won't be worth a damn when I come out of here—if I ever do.

Write when you can to your nutty old cousin.

*November 17, 1950*

Dear Ethel:

. . . Everybody is much more worried and jittery than I am. I've always thought that if I could get my hands on a would-be assassin he'd never try it again. But I guess that's impossible. The grand guards who were hurt in the attempt on me didn't have a fair chance. The one who was killed was just cold bloodedly murdered before he could do anything. But his assassin did not live but a couple of minutes—one of the S[ecret] S[ervice] men put a bullet in one ear and it came out the other. I stuck my head out the upstairs window to see what was going on. One of the guards yelled "Get back." I did, then dressed and went down stairs. I was the only calm one in the house. You see I've been shot at by experts and unless your name's on the bullet you needn't be afraid—and that of course you won't find out, so why worry.

The S.S. chief said to me "Mr. President, don't you know that when there's an Air Raid Alarm you don't run out and look up, you go for cover." I saw the point but it was over then!

Hope it won't happen again. They won't let me go walking or even cross the street on foot. I say "they" won't, but it causes them so much anguish that I conform—a hard thing for a Truman to do as you know, particularly when he could force them to do as he wants. But I want no more guards killed. . . .

*November 22, 1950*

Dear Joe [Joseph McGee, Kansas City friend]:

. . . There isn't a word of truth in that Chicago Tribune venture. You might tell the gentleman named Holmes [a *Tribune* reporter in Kansas City] that if he comes out with a pack of lies about Mrs. Truman or any of my family his hide won't hold shucks when I get through with him.

*December 20, 1950*

My dear Miss [Barbara] Heggie:

I have just read your story in the Woman's Home Companion—"What Makes Margaret Sing?"

It is lovely. Thank you from my heart. The vast majority of our people can never understand what a terrible handicap it is to a lovely girl to have her father the president of the United States.

Stuffed shirt critics and vicious political opponents of mine sometimes try to take it out on Margie. It's her dad they are after and Margie understands. You have come more nearly stating the situation in its true light than anyone who has made the attempt. . . .

Hope you'll regard this communication as one from a fond father and keep it confidential. Only my "mad" letters are published!

❦

*May 19, 1951*

Dear Ethel:

. . . When stories like this one begin to circulate the country's safe. It seems that a mental expert knocked on St. Peter's Gate and asked for admission. When the expert had stated his case and his background, Peter invited him to come right in. The old saint said that the services of such an expert were needed. He said God had been acting queerly lately and it was the consensus of the saints that the situation should be examined. God had been talking as if he thought he were MacArthur. . . .

❦

*June 25, 1951*

Dear Bess:

. . . This week contains another very important—most important—anniversary. Thursday will be thirty-two years! I've never been anything but happy for that anniversary. Maybe I haven't given you all you're entitled to, but I've done my best, and I'm still in love with the prettiest girl in the world. . . .

*January 28, 1952*

Dear Dave [Morgan, Kansas friend and former business partner]:

. . . The State Department is a peculiar organization, made up principally of extremely bright people who made tremendous college marks but who have had very little association with actual people down to the ground. They are clannish and snooty and sometimes I feel like firing the whole bunch but it requires a tremendous amount of education to accomplish the purposes for which the State Department is set up. . . .

The present secretary of state [Dean Acheson] is one of the best that has ever been in the office, but on lower levels we still have the career men who have been taken out of the colleges without any experience with the common people. I'll give you one particular instance to show you just how the situation works.

Alben Barkley, when he was United States senator, was in Egypt with a bunch of congressmen and senators on a parliamentary union meeting. The Charge d'affaires in Cairo escorted them. He wore a checked suit, carried a cane, wore a cap, and talked with an Oxford accent. Barkley kept looking at him and wondering if the gentleman could have been reared in Egypt. Finally he asked him what his antecedents were. The man said he was a native of Topeka, Kansas.

Of course, if he dared go back to Topeka wearing that checked suit, the cap, and carrying a cane, he would have lasted about ten minutes in the Kansas Hotel lobby. . . .

❧

*May 11, 1952*

Dear Ethel:

. . . Of course I can't be there [a relative's wedding], much to my regret. . . . You know what would happen if I came? The wedding would be so submerged in the visit of the President that the young people wouldn't know they'd had a wedding. First, advance secret service men would "case the joint"—house or church, wherever it takes place. They have to have the guest list and be sure no one of them had a knife, a gun or a bomb. They'd be stationed at every corner of the house or church and the whole town police force would be on duty and as jittery as if the Russian Army were coming. So you can see it would spoil the event. . . .

❧

*Feburary 2, 1952*

Dear Ethel:

. . . I had an experience with Winthrop Aldrich, son in law of John D. Rockefeller, while I was in the Senate. I was making an investigation of a company with an account in the Chase National Bank. The vice president (and there are forty or fifty of them) who gave me the information I wanted, asked me to go with him and meet Mr. Aldrich, the president. Being polite I said OK and we went to the great man's outer office. My poor V.P. fidgeted and squirmed and I being a Missourian was highly amused. Finally I said to him "You tell the old s.o.b. to go to hell. I didn't want to see him anyway." He was abject in his apologies. But when I became president of the U.S. the great Mr. Aldrich came around for an appointment. I let him cool his heels for about an hour, which I'm sure was no lesson to him, while I saw half a dozen *common* people ahead of him. Us Missourians are not vindictive, no, not at all. When he finally got in I said nothing doing to his proposition.

❧

*November* 25, 1952

Dear Nellie:

. . . Ike came to see me and he was not at all happy when he left. He found that being president is sort of a working job and Ike doesn't like to work—either mentally or physically. What a fool he is to have left "social security" in the form of lifetime pay and emoluments of a 5-star general and move into the most controversial and nerve-wracking job in the world! . . .

❧

*April* 10, 1955

Dear Dean [Acheson]:

. . . I don't want to be an "elder statesman" politician. I like being a nose buster and an ass kicker much better and reserve my serious statements for committees and schools. . . .

❧

*August* 20, 1955

Dear Margie,

. . . I'm getting letter after letter asking me to go back to 1600 Penn. Ave.—but I'm not going, and that's not saying I couldn't. Wish I could be 50 instead of 70. I'd take 'em around the bend you bet. Your mamma's in better shape than she's been since we left the Great White Jail, and I'm not going to put her to bed by going back there.

❧

*March 19, 1956*

Dear Margie:

. . . There's one thing that worried me in our phone conversation last night. You said that no one is to be trusted. Maybe your dad, who has had more contracts and experiences with people than anyone alive, [can] tell you that more than 95% of all the people can be trusted.

If you don't trust the people you love and those who work for you in all capacities you'll be the unhappiest and [most] frustrated person alive. . . .

❧

*February 11, 1958*

Dear Guy [Lombardo]:

. . . I cannot disagree with you that the Missouri Waltz may be a good piece of popular music, but in my opinion it is not a proper state song.

It is likely that I am prejudiced, but we both know that it takes a tenor, a baritone, and a bass to sing the Star Spangled Banner. I have never understood why it was not set to music that every single soldier in the Army could sing.

I always stand at attention for both songs and always with regret that I cannot appreciate the music of either of them.

September 29, 1958

Dear Justice [Edward] McFaddin [of Arkansas Supreme Court]:

. . . I've had several moments of great joy, the end of two wars shortly after my going to the White House, the end of World War I while I was firing a battery of artillery on the front at Verdun and one or two other great moments—the election night of 1948 for instance—but the greatest joy of them all was when my sweetheart from six years old on consented to become Mrs. Truman after World War I. She'd have been willing before the War but I thought I might be legless, eyeless, or under some other handicap and we put it off until June 28th, 1919—just as soon as we could make arrangements after my discharge on May 6, 1919. When my daughter came that topped it.

My moments of greatest sorrow were when my mother and father passed away and when I had to officiate at the burial of some of my soldiers in World War I.

To contemplate changes for the past I think is an idle pastime. I've had a grand and full life from beginning to now. I like to look to the future and use the experiences of the past for its improvement. Wish I could live another 50 years at least and have a hand in the greatest future any Republic ever contemplated. . . .

# *Dear Diary*

Truman continually jotted notes to himself on events of the day, large and small. The sum of these jottings is a lively, revealing diary.

*April 12, 1945*

. . . I am not easily shocked but was certainly shocked when I was told of the president's death and the weight of the government had fallen on my shoulders.

. . . I decided the best thing to do was to go home and get as much rest as possible and face the music. . . .

*5/27/45*

. . . We had a picture show tonight. Jeanette MacDonald in "Springtime." Everybody including me cried a little—so they all enjoyed the show.

6/1/45

. . . I'm always so lonesome when the family leaves. I have no one to raise a fuss over my neckties and my haircuts, my shoes and my clothes generally. I usually put on a terrible tie . . . just to get a loud protest from Bess & Margie. When they are gone I have to put on the right one and it's no fun. . . .

6/5/45

Another hectic day in the executive office. Saw a lot of customers. Hope they all left happy. Most of 'em did. . . .

Got back to the White House at 10:30. Called the Madam and talked to her and my baby girl (who doesn't like that designation). I can't help wanting to talk to my sweetheart and my baby every night. I'm a damn fool I guess because I could never get excited or worked up about gals or women. I only had one sweetheart from the time I was six. . . .

6/17/45

. . . I have to decide Japanese strategy—shall we invade Japan proper or shall we bomb and blockade? That is my hardest decision to date. But I'll make it when I have all the facts. . . .

7/7/45

. . . A couple of nice children gave me a plaque commemorating $715,000,000.00 on bond sales by the school children. The nice boy made me a speech. At his age, I would surely have passed out, if I had had to make a statement similar to his, to the town mayor, let alone the president of the United States. He did not seem to be much bothered or impressed. These modern kids are something to write home about, even if they cannot spell or find a word in the dictionary or tell what 3 x 3 equals. . . .

❧

7/25/45

. . . We have discovered the most terrible bomb in the history of the world. It may be the fire destruction prophesied in the Euphrates Valley Era, after Noah and his fabulous Ark. . . .

This weapon is to be used against Japan between now and August 10th. I have told the Sec. of War, Mr. Stimson, to use it so that military objectives and soldiers and sailors are the target and not women and children. Even if the Japs are savages, ruthless, merciless, and fanatic, we as the leader of the world for the common welfare cannot drop this terrible bomb on the old capital or the new [Kyoto, Tokyo].

He & I are in accord. The target will be a purely military one and we will issue a warning statement asking the Japs to surrender and save lives. I'm sure they will not do that, but we will have given them the chance. It is certainly a good thing for the world that Hitler's crowd or Stalin's did not discover this atomic bomb. It seems to be the most terrible thing ever discovered, but it can be made the most useful. . . .

❧

*9/20/47*

. . . There were several thousand people at the airport in Paducah [Kentucky], all of whom wanted to see Jumbo, the Cardiff Giant, the president of the United States. It is a most amazing spectacle, this worship of high office. . . .

❧

*mid-12/47*

. . . I have just made some additions to my Kitchen Cabinet, which I shall pass on to my successor in case the Cow should fall down when she goes over the moon.

I appointed a Secretary for Inflation. I have given him the worry of convincing the people that no matter how high the prices go, nor how low wages become, there just is not any danger to things temporal or eternal. I am of the opinion that he will take a real load off my mind—if Congress does not.

Then I have appointed a Secretary of Reaction. I want him to abolish flying machines and tell me how to restore oxcarts, oar boats, and sailing ships. What a load he can take off my mind if he will put the atom back together so it cannot be broken up. . . .

I have appointed a Secretary for Columnists. His duties are to listen to all radio commentators, read all columnists in the newspapers from ivory tower to lowest gossip, coordinate them, and give me the result so I can run the United States and the World as it should be. I have several able men in reserve besides the present holder of the job, because I think in a week or two the present Secretary for Columnists will need the services of a psychiatrist . . .

I have appointed a Secretary of Semantics—a most important post. He is to furnish me 40 to 50 dollar words. Tell me how to say yes and no in the same sentence without a contradiction. He is to tell me the combination of words that will put me against inflation in San Francisco and for it in New York. He is to show me how to keep silent—and say everything. You can very well see how he can save me an immense amount of worry. . . .

❧

*1/6/48*

Congress meets—Too bad too.

They'll do nothing but wrangle, pull phony investigations, and generally upset the affairs of the nation.

I'm to address them soon. They won't like the address either.

❧

*2/2/48*

I sent the Congress a civil rights message. They no doubt will receive it as coldly as they did my State of the Union message. But it needs to be said.

❧

*2/8/48*

I go for a walk and go to church. The preacher always treats me as a church member and not as the head of a circus. That's the reason I go to the 1st Baptist church.

One time I went to the Foundry Methodist Church, next door to the 1st Baptist, because Rev. Harris was Chaplain for the Senate when I was V.P. He made a real show of the occasion. I'll never go back. I don't go to church for show. I hate headline hunters and showmen as a class and individually. It's too bad I'm not a showman. My predecessor was, and I suppose profited politically by it. Fate put me here, and fate can keep me here or put me out—and out would suit me better.

*2/14/48*

. . . My "baby" and her best friend gave me valentines as does Bess, and I couldn't get out to get them one.

In times past I was the giver; now things are reversed, and I'm the givee. It's hell to be the Chief of State!

*7/16/48*

. . . {Thomas} Dewey synthetically milks cows and pitches hay for the cameras just as that other fakir, Teddy Roosevelt, did . . . I don't believe the USA wants any more fakirs—Teddy and Franklin are enough. So I'm going to make a common sense, intellectually honest campaign. It will be a novelty—and it will win.

*9/14/48*

Another hell of a day. I'm sitting for an old Polish painter, and I don't like to pose—but it's also a part of the trial of being president. He's painted a nice stuffed shirt picture. This is about No. 7 or No. 8. Hope it's the last. . . .

❧

*11/1/49*

. . . Had dinner by myself tonight. Worked in the Lee House office until dinner time. A butler came in very formally and said, "Mr. President, dinner is served." I walk into the dining room in the Blair House. Barnett in tails and white tie pulls out my chair, pushes me up to the table. John in tails and white tie brings me a fruit cup. Barnett takes away the empty cup. John brings me a plate, Barnett brings me a tenderloin, John brings me asparagus, Barnett brings me carrots and beets. I have to eat alone and in silence in candle-lit room. I ring. Barnett takes the plate and butter plates. John comes in with a napkin and silver crumb tray—there are no crumbs but John has to brush them off the table anyway. Barnett brings me a plate with a finger bowl and doily on it. I remove the finger bowl and doily and John puts a glass saucer and a little bowl on the plate. Barnett brings me some chocolate custard. John brings me a demitasse (at home a little cup of coffee—about two good gulps) and my dinner is over. I take a hand bath in the finger bowl and go back to work.

What a life!

❧

*6/30/50*

[Army Secretary] Frank Pace called me at 5 A.M. E.D.T I was already up and shaved. Said MacArthur wanted two divisions of ground troops. Authorized a regiment to be used . . .

What will that do to Mao Tse-tung we don't know. Must be careful not to cause a general Asiatic war. Russia is figuring on an attack in the Black Sea and toward the Persian Gulf. Both prizes Moscow has wanted since Ivan the Terrible. . . .

*8/15/50*

A prayer said over & over all my life from eighteen years old and younger.

Oh! Almighty and Everlasting God, Creator of Heaven, Earth, and the Universe.

Help me to be, to think, to act what is right, because it is right; make me truthful, honest, and honorable in all things; make me intellectually honest, for the sake of right and honor and without thought of reward to me. Give me the ability to be charitable, forgiving, and patient with my fellowmen—help me to understand their motives and their shortcomings—even as Thou understandest mine!

Amen, Amen, Amen.

*12/9/50*

Margie held a concert here in D.C. on Dec. 5th. It was a good one. She was well accompanied by a young pianist name of Allison, whose father is a Baptist preacher in Augusta, Georgia. Young Allison played two pieces after the intermission, one of which was the great A flat Chopin Waltz Opus 42. He did it as well as it could be done and I've heard Paderewski, Moritz Rosenthal, and Joseph Lhévinne play it.

A frustrated critic on the Washington Post wrote a lousy review. The only thing, General Marshall said, he didn't criticize was the varnish on the piano. He put my "baby"as low as he could and he made the young accompanist look like a dub.

It upset me and I wrote him what I thought of him. I told him he is lower than [Westbrook] Pegler and that was intended to be an insult worse than a reflection on his ancestry. I would never reflect on a man's mother because mothers are not to be attacked although mine has!

Well I've had a grand time this day. I've been accused of putting my "baby"who is the "apple of my eye"in a bad position. I don't think that she is. She doesn't either—thank the Almighty.

In addition to personal matters I've had conference after conference on the jittery situation facing the country. [Clement] Attlee, Formosa, Communist China, Chiang Kai-shek, Japan, Germany, France, India, etc. I've worked for peace for five years and six months and it looks like World War III is here.

I hope not—but we must meet whatever comes—and we will.

❧

*2/20/52*

. . . The "Boss" and I had breakfast at 8:30 and about 8:50 I went to the White House office. Since the assault on the police and the secret service, I ride across the street in a car the roof of which will turn a grenade, the windows and sides turn a bullet, and floor will stop a land mine! Behind me in an open car ride six or seven men with automatics and machineguns. The uniformed police stop traffic in every direction—and I cross the street in state and wonder why anyone would want to live like that. When I take my morning walk at 7 A.M. a guard walks beside me and he's always a fine man and a congenial conversationalist. Behind me are three more good men, athletes and good shots, across the street is another good man, and a half block behind me is a car with maybe five or six well equipped guards. It is a hell of a way to live. But after the assault on Blair House I learned that the men who want to keep me alive are the ones who get hurt and not the president. I'd always thought that I might be able to take care of an assassin as old Andy Jackson did but I found that the guards get hurt and not the president. So now I conform to rules without protest. . . .

❧

*6/1/52*

A couple of golden crowns with all kinds of expensive jewels have been stolen from a Roman Catholic shrine in Brooklyn. The crowns were on images of Jesus Christ and Mary his mother.

I've an idea if Jesus were here his sympathies would be with the thieves and not with the Pharisees who crowned him with gold and jewels.

The only crown he ever wore was one of thorns placed there by emissaries of the Roman emperor and Jewish priesthood. He came to help the lowly and the down trodden. But since Constantine the Great he has been taken over by the Despots of both Church and State. . . .

❧

*11/20/52*

The president elect [Eisenhower] came to see me day before yesterday, Nov 18 '52. When he came into the president's office he had a chip on his shoulder. . . .

I told him when he came into the presidential office that all I had in mind is an orderly turnover to him. . . . I offered to leave the pictures of Hidalgo, the Mexican Liberator, given to me for the presidential office, San Martin, given to me by the Argentine Government, and Bolívar, given to me by the Venezuelan Government, in the president's office. I was informed, very curtly, that I'd do well to take them with me—that the governments of these countries would, no doubt, give the new president the same pictures! Then I gave him the world globe that he used in World War II which he had given me at Frankfurt when I went to Potsdam. He accepted that—not very graciously. . . .

❧

*5/20/53*
*Independence*

This morning at 7 A.M. I took off for my morning walk. . . .

I went on down Van Horn Road (some call it Truman Road now) and took a look at the work progressing on the widening for a two way traffic line through the county seat. . . . The boss or the contractor was looking on and I asked him if he didn't need a good strawboss. He took a look at me and then watched the work a while and then took another look and broke out in a broad smile and said "Oh yes! You *are* out of a job aren't you."

❧

*7/8/53*

I went walking this morning as I usually do when the weather permits and my mail reading is not overwhelming. . . .

As I walked out of the alley into Delaware Street a young man jumped [out] of his car on the west side of the street and said that he and his wife had been waiting for a chance to see me. He was from [Streator] Ill. . . . , said he'd seen me from the station there on my campaign tour. He was a nice looking man and his wife was a pretty young woman. Both looked sleepy. They'd evidently arisen early so as to be sure they had a chance to see me and shake hands.

I always try to be as pleasant as I can to the numerous people who want to see and talk to me. They, of course, don't know that I walk early to get a chance to think over things and get ready for work of the day. But they come from every state in the union and I must consider that they've made a special effort to see me—so I treat them accordingly even [if] it sometimes does spoil a train of thought. . . .



*2/2/55*

. . . When the Gates of Heaven are reached by the shades of the earth bound, the rank and riches enjoyed on this planet won't be of value. Some of our grandees will have to do a lot of explaining on how they got that way. Wish I could hear their alibis! I can't, for the probabilities are I'll be thinking up some for myself. . . .

6/56
*London*

. . . Visited the Mauritzhaus, a small art gallery in the Hague. It has some Rembrandts and some of the best of the Dutch landscape painters. These Dutch painters of portraits and landscapes were artists and geniuses.

They make our modern day daubers and frustrated ham and egg men look just what they are. It is too bad that our age has forgotten those things that make real art appealing—or they are too lazy to take the pains to do real work.

I saw a bronze monstrosity in one of the art galleries and asked the director if it was meant to be a bronze picture of a devil's darning needle, a vicious-looking bug that's scary to look at. The director turned pale and told me it was a modernist conception of love at first sight. Then *I* fainted. . . .

❧

*1/21/60*

. . . While looking over the death notices of the Washington Post and the N.Y. Times along with those at home in the K. C. Star and the Independence Examiner, I began to think about what those notices mean to the descendants.

The children of the people who are in the death notices try to show just how good the former generation were. It is a great thing, for most second generations are sure that the preceding one undoubtedly was as ignorant and inefficient as could be.

But—when the older generation passed on, the descendants began to do a little thinking and wishing that great things had happened.

# *Press Relations*

*I like the press conference. I have a great time with the press people, and I usually find out more from them than they did from me.*

---

*A press conference is kind of a show, and one of the best there is in Washington.*

—HARRY TRUMAN

❧

*January 31, 1946*

REPORTER: Mr. President, do you support the State Department's policy that the United States should—

PRESIDENT TRUMAN: The State Department doesn't have a policy unless I support it.

❧

*Feburary 28, 1947*

REPORTER: You are quoted as having said at the last Congressional reception that there are only four [Republicans] you didn't like.

PRESIDENT TRUMAN: Well, I don't remember that comment. . . .

REPORTER: Would it be only four, Mr. President?

PRESIDENT TRUMAN: Well, I wouldn't like to limit it to four.

❦

*April 3, 1947*

REPORTER: Mr. President, have you given any thought to grocery prices?

PRESIDENT TRUMAN: I have given it no thought. Only when I go to pay my bill.

❦

*September 2, 1948*

REPORTER: Mr. President, Governor Dewey said yesterday that cleaning the communists out of Washington was a national job of great urgency, and one that should be tackled as soon as a Republican president could get it done. Any comment on that?

PRESIDENT TRUMAN: . . . I think Mr. Dewey's intention is to eliminate the Democrats from government, not the communists.

❦

*December 2, 1948*

REPORTER: Mr. President, to go back to lobbyists, would you be against lobbyists who are working for your program?

PRESIDENT TRUMAN: Well, that's a different matter. We probably wouldn't call these people lobbyists. We would call them citizens appearing in the public interest.

❦

*February 10, 1949*

REPORTER: Mr. President, Mr. Dewey was lamenting the fact that the Republican Party is split wide open. Do you have any advice for him that would—

PRESIDENT TRUMAN: I gave him all the advice I possibly could during the campaign.

❦

*March 3, 1949*

REPORTER: Mr. President, would you name the special interests to which you made reference several times, sir?

PRESIDENT TRUMAN: It would not be difficult to name them, Joe [Short], but then I don't think I need to name them for a reporter of the *Baltimore Sun*. They know the special interests and support them all the time.

❦

*April 7, 1949*

REPORTER: Your first four years will be up on the 12th. Is there any comment you would like to make on your first four years as President?

PRESIDENT TRUMAN: I always say the first four years are the hardest.

❦

*June 16, 1949*

REPORTER: Mr. President, the first thing Jefferson did was to release eleven newspaper publishers from prison.

PRESIDENT TRUMAN: Yes. I think he made a mistake on that.

❧

*March 30, 1950*

REPORTER: Do you think that Senator McCarthy can show any disloyalty exists in the State Department?

PRESIDENT TRUMAN: I think the greatest asset that the Kremlin has is Senator McCarthy.

❧

*April 13, 1950*

REPORTER: Mr. President, Senator Taft said this week that you had libeled Senator McCarthy. Would you care to make any comment?

PRESIDENT TRUMAN: Do you think that is possible?

❧

*April 17, 1952*

REPORTER: To what do you attribute the fact that newspaper editors polled are pretty bad in picking presidential winners.

PRESIDENT TRUMAN: I will tell you exactly what is the matter with them. They don't know anything about politics.

❧

*January 15, 1953*

PRESIDENT TRUMAN: . . . It might be interesting to you to know that since 1945, when I came up here to the White House, I have taken a thousand and two morning walks. Some of you went on one or two, but you didn't go on any more. . . .

I want to say to you people that I do really appreciate the privilege I have had of becoming acquainted with all of you, of talking to you frankly as best I can, and answering your questions straight from the shoulder. . . . I get as much kick out of these things as you have.

I hope all of you have a happy and prosperous time from now on, and that you will have just as much fun with my successor as you have with me.

REPORTER: Mr. President—[warm and prolonged applause for the president]. Thank you!

# *My Fellow Americans*

*6/28/45*
*University of Kansas City*

The night before last, I arrived in Salt Lake City, Utah, at 10 P.M. from San Francisco, which I had left on the same time schedule at 8 P.M. I left Salt Lake City the next morning after breakfast . . . and arrived in Kansas City, Missouri, in exactly three hours and a half.

My grandfather made that trip time and again from 1846 to 1854, and again from 1864 to 1870, and when he made that trip it took him exactly 3 months to go, and 3 months to come back.

That is the age we in which we live. The time is coming when that trip, in my opinion, will be made in one hour and a half, instead of three hours and a half. The time is coming when we will be transporting the freight of the world, and the express of the world, and the mail of the world on a schedule that will be almost up with travel of the earth in its turn on its axis. . . .

I am anxious to bring home to you that the world is no longer county-size, no longer state-size, no longer nation-size. It is one world. . . . It is a world in which we must all get along.

*10/3/45*
*to Congress*

The discovery of the means of releasing atomic energy began a new era in the history of civilization. The scientific and industrial knowledge on which this discovery rests does not relate merely to another weapon. It may some day prove to be more revolutionary in the development of human society than the invention of the wheel, the use of metals, or the steam or internal combustion engine. . . .

The release of atomic energy constitutes a new force too revolutionary to consider in the framework of old ideas.

*1/7/48*
*to Congress*

We are rightly proud of the high standards of medical care we know how to provide in the United States. The fact is, however, that most of our people cannot afford to pay for the care they need.

I have often and strongly urged that this condition demands a national health program. The heart of the program must be a national system of payment for medical care based on well-tried insurance principles. This great nation cannot afford to allow its citizens to suffer needlessly from the lack of proper medical care.

❧

*6/12/48*
*University of California, Berkeley*

I have a little hesitation about addressing this august body, shall I say, everybody with degrees emeritus and all the other $40 words that go with an education. The only degree that I ever earned was at George Washington University in Washington, D.C. My daughter went to school there for four years and earned me a degree.

❧

*9/18/48*
*Dexter, Iowa*

I heard a fellow tell a story about how he felt when he had to make speeches. . . . He said when he has to make a speech, he felt like the fellow who was at the funeral of his wife, and the undertaker had asked him if he would ride down to the cemetery in the same car with his mother-in-law. He said, "Well, I can do it, but it's just going to spoil the whole day for me."

❧

*9/20/48, Denver*
*Colorado*

Republicans in Washington have a habit of becoming curiously deaf to the voice of the people. They have a hard time hearing what the ordinary people of the country are saying. But they have no trouble at all hearing what Wall Street is saying. They are able to catch the slightest whisper from big business and the special interests.

*9/21/48*
*Provo, Utah*

Two-thirds of you stayed at home 2 years ago, and look what you got. You elected the 80th Congress, and you got just what you deserved; and I don't feel sorry for you about it either. If you do the same thing next time you won't have anybody but yourselves to blame.

*9/23/48*
*Merced, California*

The Republican policy is to let the big fellow get the big incomes, and let a little of it trickle down off the table like the crumbs fell to Lazarus.

*9/23/48*
*Fresno, California*

You have got a terrible Congressman [Bertrand W. Gearhart] here in this district. He is one of the worst. He is one of the worst obstructionists in the Congress. He has done everything he possibly could to cut the throats of the farmer and the laboringman. If you send him back, that will be your fault if you get your own throat cut.

I am speaking plainly these days. I am telling you facts. Nobody else will tell 'em to you. . . .

You don't have to worry about where I stand. You know! I want you to see whether you can find out where the opposition stands. I'll bet you can't.

❧

10/14/48
*Madison, Wisconsin*

I remember about 20 years ago that a popular Republican slogan was, "Two cars in every garage." This year their slogan is, "Two families in every garage."

❧

10/26/48
*Cleveland, Ohio*

These polls that the Republican candidate is putting out are like sleeping pills designed to lull the voters into sleeping on election day. You might call them sleeping polls.

You know that the same doctor I told you about in Pittsburgh the other night—that Republican candidate—keeps handing out these sleeping polls, and a lot of people have been taking them. The doctor keeps telling the people: "Don't worry. Take a poll and go to sleep."

Most of the people are not going to be lulled to sleep or be fooled. They know that sleeping polls are bad for the system. They affect the mind and the body. An overdose could be fatal—can so affect your mind that your body will be too lazy to go to the polls on election day. "You don't need to vote, the election is won—all I have to do is get Truman out of the White House."

❧

2/24/49

*Jefferson-Jackson Day Dinner, Washington, D.C.*

Once upon a time, there were a number of citizens who thought that Andrew Jackson ought to have a suitable coffin. At great expense, they went to Syria and purchased a marble sarcophagus. A sarcophagus, as you know, is a tomb—a big marble coffin with a marble lid. These citizens then shipped this marble box to Washington, which was quite a job as it weighed four or five tons.

At last, they thought, a suitable resting place had been provided for Andrew Jackson.

Well, the only trouble with the project was that Andrew Jackson wasn't dead. Moreover, he wasn't ready to die. And he did not intend to be hurried to his grave.

Courteously but firmly he wrote to these well-meaning citizens, and said, "I must decline the intended honor."

And they never did get Old Hickory into that thing. You can still see it, if you're interested, out in front of the Smithsonian Institution. It still sits there. Andy wouldn't even be buried in it.

I think that this little story has a moral in it. It is this: Before you offer to bury a good Democrat, you better be sure he is dead.

❧

5/12/50

*Missoula, Montana*

You know, some people will take a look at an acorn and all they can see is just an acorn. But people of [Congressman] Mike

Mansfield's type are something different. They can see into the future. They can see a giant oak tree, with its great limbs spreading upward and outward coming from that acorn.

In Washington, there are some men, no matter how hard they try, who can only see little acorns. . . . Even give them a magnifying glass, or even a pair of spyglasses, or even a telescope, they just shake their heads and all they can say is, "I'm sorry, I can't see anything but an acorn there."

❧

10/25/50
*National Guard Association, Washington, D.C.*

I pinned a medal on General MacArthur the other day, and told him I wished I had a medal like that, and he said that it was my duty to give the medals, not to receive them. That is always the way. About all I receive are the bricks. It's a good thing I have got a pretty hard head, or it would have been broken a long time ago.

❧

12/17/52
*Wright Memorial Dinner, Washington, D.C.*

One of the results of this system is that it gives the president a good many hot potatoes to handle—but the president gets a lot of hot potatoes from every direction anyhow, and a man who can't handle them has no business in that job. That makes me think of a saying that I used to hear from my old friend and colleague on the Jackson County Court. He said, "Harry, if you can't stand the heat you better get out of the kitchen."

❧

*1/15/53*
*the White House*

Next Tuesday, General Eisenhower will be inaugurated as president of the United States. A short time after the new president takes his oath of office, I will be on the train going back home to Independence, Missouri. I will once again be a plain, private citizen of this great republic.

That is as it should be. Inauguration Day will be a great demonstration of our democratic process. I am glad to be part of it—glad to wish General Eisenhower all possible success, as he begins his term—glad the whole world will have a chance to see how simply and how peacefully our American system transfers the vast power of the presidency from my hands to his. . . .

I want to say "goodbye" and "thanks for your help." And I want to talk to you a little while about what has happened since I became your president. . . .

I suppose that history will remember my term in office as the years when the "cold war" began to overshadow our lives. I have had hardly a day in office that has not been dominated by this all-embracing struggle—this conflict between those who love freedom and those who would lead the world back into slavery and darkness. And always in the background there has been the atomic bomb.

But when history says that my term of office saw the beginning of the cold war, it will also say that in those 8 years we have set the course that can win it. We have succeeded in carving out a new set of policies to attain peace—positive policies, policies of world leadership, policies that express faith in other free people. We have averted World War III up to now, and we may already have succeeded in establishing conditions which can keep that war from happening as far ahead as man can see. . . .

As the free world grows stronger, more united, more attractive to men on both sides of the Iron Curtain—and as the Soviet hopes for easy expansion are blocked—then there will have to come a time of change in the Soviet world. Nobody can say for sure when that is going to be, or exactly how it will come about, whether by revolution, or trouble in the satellite states, or by a change inside the Kremlin.

Whether the communist rulers shift their policies of their own free will—or whether the change comes about in some other way—I have not a doubt in the world that a change will occur. . . .

We have made progress in spreading the blessing of American life to all of our people. There has been a tremendous awakening of the American conscience on the great issues of civil rights—equal economic opportunities, equal rights of citizenship, and equal educational opportunities for all our people, whatever their race or religion or status of birth.

So, as I empty the drawers of this desk, and as Mrs. Truman and I leave the White House, we have no regret. We feel we have done our best in the public service. I hope and believe we have contributed to the welfare of this nation and to the peace of the world.

# *Bibliography*

The following bibliography lists key sources consulted in the preparation of this volume.

Acheson, Dean. 1969. *Present at the Creation: My Years in the State Department*. London: Hamish Hamilton.

Adler, Bill, ed. 1966. *Presidential Wit from Washington to Johnson*. New York: Trident Press.

Allen, George E. 1950. *Presidents Who Have Known Me*. New York: Simon and Schuster.

Aurthur, Robert Alan. 1971. "The Wit and Sass of Harry S. Truman." *Esquire*, August.

———. 1971. "Harry Truman Chuckles Dryly." *Esquire*, September.

Brembeck, Cole S. 1952. "Harry S Truman at the Whistle Stops." *Quarterly Journal of Speech*, February.

Caldwell, George S., ed. 1966. *Good Old Harry: The Wit and Wisdom of Harry S Truman*. New York: Hawthorn.

Clifford, Clark. 1991. *Counsel to the President*. New York: Random House.

Daniels, Jonathan. 1950. *The Man of Independence*. Philadelphia: Lippincott.

Donovan, Robert. 1984. *The Words of Harry Truman*. New York: Newmarket.

Ferrell, Robert H., ed. 1980. *The Autobiography of Harry S. Truman*. Boulder, CO: Colorado Associated University Press.

———, ed. 1980. *Off the Record: The Private Papers of Harry S. Truman*. New York: Harper & Row.

———, ed. 1983. *Dear Bess: The Letters from Harry to Bess Truman, 1910-1959*. New York: Norton.

———. 1984. *Truman: A Centenary Remembrance*. New York: Viking.

———, ed. 1991. *Truman in the White House: The Diary of Eben A. Ayers*. Columbia, MO: University of Missouri Press.

———, 1994. *Harry S. Truman: A Life*. Columbia, MO: University of Missouri Press.

Fields, Alonzo. 1961. *My 21 Years in the White House*. New York: Coward-McCann.

Fredericks, Vic. 1966. *The Wit and Wisdom of the Presidents*. New York: Frederick Fell.

Frost, Elizabeth. 1988. *The Bully Pulpit: Quotations from American Presidents*. New York: Facts on File.

Gallen, David, ed. 1994. *The Quotable Truman*. New York: Carroll & Graf.

Gallu, Samuel. 1975. *"Give 'Em Hell, Harry!"* New York: Dunetz & Lovett.

Goodman, Mark, ed. 1974. *Give 'Em Hell, Harry!* New York: Award.

Harnsberger, Caroline Thomas, ed. 1964. *Treasury of Presidential Quotations*. Chicago: Follett.

Hay, Peter. 1988. *All the Presidents' Ladies*. New York: Viking.

Hechler, Ken. 1982. *Working with Truman: A Personal Memoir of the White House Years*. New York: Putnam.

Henning, Chuck, ed. 1992. *The Wit and Wisdom of Politics*. Golden, CO: Fulcrum.

Hersey, John. 1980. *Aspects of the Presidency*. New Haven and New York: Ticknor & Fields.

Hillman, William. 1952. *Mr. President*. New York: Farrar, Straus and Young.

Kirkendall, Richard S., ed. 1989. *The Harry S. Truman Encyclopedia*. Boston: G. K. Hall.

Leuchtenburg, William E. 1984. "Give 'Em Harry." *The New Republic*, May 21.

Luhr, Catherine Adair. 1985. Harry S Truman and Rhetorical Presence. M.A. dissertation, University of Virginia.

McCullough, David. 1992. *Truman*. New York: Simon & Schuster.

Parker, John F. 1978. *The Fun and Laughter of Politics*. Garden City, New York: Doubleday.

Pemberton, William E. 1989. *Harry S. Truman: Fair Dealer and Cold Warrior*. Boston: Twayne.

Phillips, Cabell. 1966. *The Truman Presidency: The History of a Triumphant Succession*. New York: Macmillan.

Poen, Monte M., ed. 1982. *Strictly Personal and Confidential: The Letters Harry Truman Never Mailed*. Boston: Little, Brown.

———, ed. 1984. *Letters Home by Harry Truman*. New York: Putnam.

Robbins, Charles. 1979. *Last of His Kind: An Informal Portrait of Harry S. Truman*. New York: Morrow.

Ross, Charles. 1948. "How Truman Did It." *Collier's*, December 25.

Ross, Irwin. 1968. *The Loneliest Campaign*. New York: New American Library; Signet, 1969.

Rossiter, Clinton. 1960. *The American Presidency*. New York: Harcourt, Brace & World.

Settel, T.S., ed. 1967. *The Quotable Harry S. Truman.* Anderson, SC: Droke House; New York: Berkeley, 1975.

Simpson, James B. 1957. *Best Quotes of '54, '55, '56*. New York: Crowell.

———. 1988. *Simpson's Contemporary Quotations*. Boston: Houghton Mifflin.

Smith, Timothy, ed. 1972. *Merriman Smith's Book of Presidents: A White House Memoir*. New York: Norton.

Steinberg, Alfred. 1962. *The Man from Missouri: The Life and Times of Harry S. Truman*. New York: Putnam.

Strahan, Jerry E. 1994. *Andrew Jackson Higgins and the Boats that Won World War II*. Baton Rouge, LA: Louisiana State University Press.

terHorst, J. F., and Col. Ralph Albertazzie. 1979. *The Flying White House: The Story of Air Force One*. New York: Coward, McCann & Geohegan; Bantam, 1980.

Thompson, Kenneth W., ed. 1984. *Portraits of American Presidents: The Truman Presidency*. Lanham, MD: University Press of America.

Thomson, David S. 1973. *HST: A Pictorial Biography*. New York: Grosset & Dunlap.

Truman, Harry S. 1945–1953. *Public Papers of the Presidents of the United States. Harry S. Truman. Containing the Public Messages, Speeches and Statements of the President*. Washington, D.C.: Government Printing Office.

———. 1955. *Memoirs*. Volume 1, *Year of Decisions*. Garden City, New York: Doubleday.

———. 1956. *Memoirs*. Volume 2, *Years of Trial and Hope*. Garden City, New York: Doubleday.

———. 1960. *Mr. Citizen*. New York: Geis.

———. 1960. *Truman Speaks*. New York: Columbia University Press.

———. 1964. My First Eighty Years. *Saturday Evening Post*, June 13.

Truman, Margaret. 1973. *Harry S. Truman*. New York: Morrow.

———, ed. 1981. *Letters from Father: The Truman Family's Personal Correspondence*. New York: Arbor House.

———. 1986. *Bess W. Truman*. New York: Macmillan.

———, ed. 1989. *Where the Buck Stops: The Personal and Private Writings of Harry S. Truman*. New York: Warner.

U.S. Congress. 1973. *Memorial Services in the Congress of the United States and Tributes in Eulogy of Harry S Truman, Late a President of the United States*. Washington, D.C.: United States Government Printing Office.

Vernon, Laura, ed. 1987. *Harry Truman Slept Here*. Independence, MO: Posy.

Weddle, Dr. J. Owen. 1974. *Presidential Vignettes*. University of Texas of the Permian Basin.

West, J. B. 1973. *Upstairs at the White House.* New York: Coward, McCann & Geoghegan.

White, Eugene, and Clair Henerlider. 1954. "What Harry S. Truman Told Us About Public Speaking." *Quarterly Journal of Speech*, February.

Williams, Herbert Lee. 1984. *The Newspaperman's President—Harry S Truman*. Chicago: Nelson-Hall.

Yergin, Daniel. 1976. "Harry Truman Revived—and Revised." *New York Times Magazine*, October 24.

# Notes

Rather than cite every source that includes the same comment by Truman or information about him, only the key source or sources are cited. Sources are listed by author's last name and date of publication if necessary (followed by "a" and "b" in the order that they appear in the bibliography—if there is more than one publication by the same author in a single year). Harry Truman's public papers are cited as PP followed by the year.

## *Wilder Than Ever About Harry*

Rossiter: Rossiter 159; Ford, Reagan: Luhr 86; I never sit on a fence: PP 1948 931; Ferrell: Ferrell 1984 250; Robbins: Robbins 146; "I look just like": Goodman 173; "All over the country": Steinberg 324; Gravel: U.S. Congress 175; Truman to Ross: Steinberg 285; "As Harry Truman": Thompson 149; Sevareid: McCullough 992; Iowa speech: PP 1948 506; Illinois speech: Poen 1984 221; third speech: Phillips 215; "A robin hops": Ferrell 1980b 140; Hart: U.S. Congress 148.

## *Truman on People*

*Churchill:* Kirkendall 282; Ferrell 1994 205; Poen 1984 195; Acheson 595; *MacArthur:* Ferrell 1980b 324; Ferrell 1980b 47; *Marshall:* Truman 1989

71; Hillman 150; Ferrell 1980b 109; *Baruch:* Ferrell 1980b 87; *Brown:* Gallen 113; *Bryan:* Truman 1989 342; *Custer:* Truman 1989 284; *de Gaulle:* Poen 1984 197; *Fulbright:* Steinberg 405; *Goldwater:* Ferrell 1994 394; *Kennedy:* Kirkendall 197; *McCarthy:* Poen 1984 237; *Molotov:* Ferrell 1980b 305; *Picasso:* Ferrell 1994 398; *Rogers:* Poen 1984 98; *Stalin:* Simpson 1957 311; *Twain:* Poen 1982 30; Ferrell 1980b 228; *Webster:* Gallen 105; *Winchell:* Poen 1982 25.

PRESIDENTS

*Washington:* Gallen 84; Truman 1989 103; Gallen 79; *John Adams:* Gallen 88; Truman 1989 244; *Jefferson:* Robbins 43; Gallen 92; Truman 1956 192; *Madison:* Gallen 96; *John Quincy Adams:* Truman 1989 266; *Jackson:* Truman 1956 193; Truman 1989 295; Luhr 33; *Van Buren:* Truman 1960b 75; Truman 1989 307; *Tyler:* Gallen 107; *Polk:* Gallen 108; *Taylor:* Truman 1989 21; *Pierce:* Truman 1989 25, 11; *Lincoln:* Hillman 90; Gallen 120; Truman 1989 322; Truman 1960b 77; *Johnson:* Truman 1960b 77; Gallen 124; Truman 1960b 77; *Grant:* Truman 1964; Truman 1956 198; Truman 1989 12; *Cleveland:* Truman 1989 13; *Harrison:* Truman 1989 38; *Theodore Roosevelt:* Truman 1956 201; Truman 1989 348; Gallen 134; *Taft:* Truman 1989 15; *Wilson:* Truman 1989 15, 351, 347; Hillman 88; *Harding:* Truman 1989 201; *Coolidge:* Truman 1989 45; *Hoover:* Ferrell 1994 99; Truman 1960a 118; *Franklin Roosevelt:* Gallen 148, 149; Ferrell 1994 133; *Eisenhower:* Ferrell 1994 449–50; Kirkendall 109; Ferrell 1980b 264; Truman 1989 65, 62, 64, 68; *John F. Kennedy:* Steinberg 428; Aurthur, August 1971; Settel 97; Aurthur, August 1971; *Richard Nixon:* Kirkendall 257; Poen 1982 134; Kirkendall 257; Steinberg 425.

## *Truman on Issues*

### AMERICANS

*If you want:* Truman 1960a, 175; *The acts:* Truman 1989 126; *The United States:* Hillman 121.

### BELIEFS

*I've never:* Truman 1960b 119; *There is nothing:* Gallen 120; *My own sympathy:* Truman 1964; *I was never:* Truman 1955 236; *I am sorry:* Truman 1960a 90; *We need men:* McCullough 767; *I am not:* Hillman 221; *Good name:* Truman 1973 363.

### CAMPAIGNING

*Cut your speech:* Daniels 202; *Don't attack:* Ferrell 1980b 341; *I always:* Williams 21; *I do not:* Truman 1956 201; *You have to:* Robbins 21; *When a candidate:* Truman 1960a 154; *A man:* Truman 1960a 153–4; *If a politician:* Williams 140; *I'm not:* U.S. Congress 154; *You know:* Ferrell 1980b 403; *I never:* U.S. Congress 27, 178; *I always:* Ferrell 1980b 373; *I have:* Truman 1960a 18; *Every political battle:* Thompson 159.

### CHILDREN

*I have found:* Simpson 1988 167; *Advice to:* Truman 1960a 202; *Children nowadays:* Ferrell 1994 451; *Mama and Papa:* U.S. Congress 147; *You can still:* Steinberg 427; *I always:* Frank S. Pepper, ed., *The Wit and Wisdom of the Twentieth Century* (New York: Peter Bedrick, 1987) 117.

### CIVIL LIBERTY

*Everyone has:* Truman 1956 271; *You cannot:* PP 1948 289; *There were:* Truman 1960b 123; *I think:* Truman 1960b 111; *There is:* PP 1950 649–50.

### CIVIL RIGHTS

*Religious:* Truman 1989 126; *Whether discrimination:* PP 1948 3; *When I was:* Ferrell 1984 191; *We can:* PP 1947 312.

### COMMUNICATING

*Never use:* Ross; *The simplest words:* Truman 1960a 277; *I never use:* Luhr 52; *I always:* Truman 1955 161; *Listeners:* Brembeck; *A good speaker:* Brembeck; *Sometimes I forget:* Hillman 65; *The greatest orators:* Truman 1989 101.

### CONGRESS

*If you tell:* Settel 51; *There are:* Ferrell 1980b 201; *Some senators:* Hillman 118; *You can't:* Ferrell 1994 184; *Most of:* Truman 1955 146; *I sometimes:* Truman 1973 346.

### CONVICTION

*You don't:* PP 1948 536; *I never:* PP 1948 931; *I have:* Truman 1960a 113; *I don't:* Settel 37; *It takes:* PP 1948 819.

### CRITICISM

*It has:* PP 1952 571; *Criticism:* Hersey 83; *It is:* Ferrell 1980b 410; *When they:* Pemberton 31; *You have:* Williams 183–4; *I don't:* Williams 70.

### DECISION MAKING

*I don't:* Ferrell 1980b 145; *It is:* PP 1948 341; *You get:* U.S. Congress 4; *I've always:* Robbins 146; *As president:* Truman 1956 305; *I made:* Truman 1960a 264; Truman 1960a 264; *I asked:* U.S. Congress 98; *Once I had:* Truman 1964; *I was:* Ferrell 1984 170; *If you've:* Ferrell 1984 170; *Looking back:* Truman 1960a 262; *The most dangerous:* Truman 1960a 261; *I have never:* Truman 1960a 97; *I never:* Phillips 12; *If you are:* Truman 1960a 265.

DEMOCRACY

*Half the fun:* Settel 128–9; *No government:* PP 1947 177; *The people:* Truman 1960a 27; *There is:* Hillman 13.

DICTATORSHIP

*Justice Brandeis:* Truman 1960a 223; *Whenever:* Truman 1960b 51; *A dictatorship:* Daniels 285; *There is:* Ferrell 1994 251.

ECONOMICS

*It's a recession:* Frost 70; *I was: New York Times,* April 14, 1985; *You know:* New York *World Telegram and Sun,* April 12, 1958; *Budget figures:* Acheson 492; *More misinformation:* Truman 1956 42; *There is nothing:* Kirkendall 130; *We believe:* Truman 1960a 299; *Taxation:* Truman 1956 41; *The danger:* Gallen 27; *[Tight money]*: Caldwell 54; *There is nothing:* Kirkendall 130; *We must never:* Hillman 83.

EDUCATION

*Education is:* PP 1948 328; *It makes:* Ferrell 1980b 167; *I can:* Ferrell 1980b 167; *I think:* Hillman 45–6.

ETHICS

*Since a child:* Poen 1984 204; *If I think:* Kirkendall 287; *It's like:* Robbins 73; *Wrongdoers:* Hillman 204; *I can:* Truman 1973 323; *There are:* Ferrell 1980b 305; *Do your duty:* Truman 1973 581.

FINE ARTS

*I know:* Ferrell 1980b 311; *I dislike:* Ferrell 1980b 299; *Did you ever:* Pemberton 6; *I don't like:* Hillman 203.

### FITNESS

*You can't:* Hersey 48; *After you:* Truman 1960a 87–8; *If you:* Truman 1960a 87; *I walk:* Hillman 133; *All my life:* Truman 1964.

### GOVERNMENT

*I think:* Adler 171; *We have:* Hillman 149; *The least:* Gallen 32; *It has been:* Donovan 28; *I think:* Hillman 235; *We would:* Adler 187; *The convention system:* Truman 1956 204; *I am against:* Truman 1960a 154–5; *A national:* Truman 1960a 227–8.

### HEALTH CARE

*When we:* Ferrell 1980b 165–6; *I am:* Kirkendall 251; *I usually:* Truman 1956 17; *I have:* Poen 1982 96.

### HIMSELF

*I'm just:* Settel 130; *I'm a:* U.S. Congress 116, 170; *I've been:* Truman 1964; *I like to gossip:* Hillman 30; *I like people:* Truman 1960a 155; *I'm a damned:* Ferrell 1980b 209; *I could hardly:* Ferrell 1980b 209; *I have been accused:* Truman 1960a 20; *I used to watch:* Truman 1955 124–5; *If my mother:* Truman 1960b 81; *There was:* McCullough 99; *It's been:* Pemberton 8; *I never:* Steinberg 215; *I have always said:* Gallen xv; *I'm not a scholar:* Robbins 42; *If I couldn't:* Hillman 204.

### HISTORY

*While still:* Truman 1955 119; *There is:* Hillman 81; *You must:* Hillman 10; *Most of the problems:* Truman 1956 1; *Our American:* Hillman 94; *Men make:* Truman 1973 52.

## HUMAN NATURE

*In reading:* Hillman 190; *There are:* Hillman 61; *Men often:* Hillman 229; *There is:* Ferrell 1980b 177; *When an:* Ferrell 1980b 323; *All of us:* Ferrell 1980b 194; *Happiness:* Hillman 195; *There's nothing:* Hersey 45; *The human animal has:* Truman 1960a 131; *The human animal and:* Ferrell 1980b 99; *Our tribal:* McCullough 942.

## HUMAN RELATIONS

*Always be:* Truman 1973 367; *Haven't you:* McCullough 410; *About the:* PP 1950 359.

## INTERNATIONAL RELATIONS

*International relations:* PP 1947 166; *No nation:* Settel 89; *Isolationism:* PP 475; *No country:* PP 1946 188; *Americans are:* Ferrell 1980b 44–5; *We in America:* Truman 1956 61; *In all:* Ferrell 1984 174; *The American approach:* Truman 1956 238; *I have never:* Truman 1973 384; *All sorts:* Truman 1960b 84; *The top dog:* Daniels 336.

## LEADERSHIP

*You can't:* Truman 1989 80; *Not all:* Ferrell 1980a 115; *A successful:* White and Henerlider; *My definition:* Gallen 46; *Leadership:* Henning 123; *I am willing:* Ferrell 1980b 134; *Keep working:* Ferrell 1980a 120; *You can always:* PP 1949 546; *It is:* Hillman 18.

## MARRIAGE

*I don't:* Hillman 153; *A man:* Truman 1973 74; *When a man:* Ferrell 1983 480.

## THE MILITARY

*{The armed forces}:* Steinberg 142; *If there:* Truman 1956 444; *One reason:* Truman 1956 444; *The professional:* Truman 1989 55; *They're honorable:* Caldwell 33; *All the generals:* Gallen 126; *Most generals:* Truman 1989 21;

*The only:* Gallen 126; *I think:* Gallen 127; *(Eisenhower): New York Times,* January 15, 1981; *The air boys:* Ferrell 1984 181; *The Marine Corps: Time,* September 18, 1950; *I know:* McCullough 528.

### MISCELLANY

*One of:* Hillman 104; *I don't: Time,* February 10, 1958; *They (the FBI):* Ferrell 1980b 22; *(Autograph seekers):* New York *World Telegram and Sun,* April 12, 1958; *(Souvenir hunters):* Vernon 7; *I've found:* Williams 177; *An economist:* McCullough 558; *A consultant:* Truman 1973 552; *Dignitaries:* Ferrell 1980b 138; *California crackpots:* Ferrell 1980b 128; *(Nevada):* Kirkendall 225.

### NATIONALITIES

*It was said:* Vernon 7; *The ancestor worshipers:* Poen 1982 147; *The Chinese:* Frost 32; *Russians:* Kirkendall 33; *Russia:* Ferrell 1980b 333; *(The Russians):* Ferrell 1994 249; *You never saw:* Steinberg 259.

### NATIVE AMERICANS

*Many of:* Truman 1989 282; *The treatment:* Gallen 69; *How would I:* Gallen 60; *There were:* Truman 1989 285; *The Indians:* Truman 1989 285; *They weren't:* Truman 1989 282; *Some of the:* Truman 1989 282; *I have always:* Truman 1960a 175.

### OLD AGE

*As you:* Settel 44; *It is remarkable:* Ferrell 1980b 294; *At 79:* McCullough 982; *I don't like:* Ferrell 1980b 408.

### PEACE

*I'd rather:* PP 1948 679; *We must find:* McCullough 785; *We must face:* PP 1945 405; *It only takes:* Settel 174; *I don't believe:* PP 1948 859; *We can well:* Settel 126.

### PERSONAL PREFERENCES

*I've got:* PP 1951 203; *I never had:* Settel 80; *I've never had:* Truman 1964; *I have never cared:* Truman 1960a 102; *My favorite animal:* Truman 1960a 39; *Most people:* Hersey 33–4.

### PHILOSOPHY

*I am inclined:* Truman 1960a 97; *I grew up:* Truman 1960a 97; *I have never:* Thomson 9; *You must watch:* Truman 1960b 113; *Three things:* U.S. Congress 4; *I don't care:* Truman 1960b 113; *Do your best:* U.S. Congress 130.

### POLITICAL INTEGRITY

*Lies:* Poen 1984 252; *Politics force:* Hillman 189; *Wherever:* Hersey 42; *An honest:* Ferrell 1984 249; *I would have:* Hillman 197; *I would much rather:* Ferrell 1980b 309.

### POLITICAL PARTIES

*I think:* Truman 1960a 113; *There is:* Truman 1960a 159; *Never in:* Gallen 83; *{The Democratic Party}:* Truman 1964; *The Republicans:* Truman 1964; *When a leader:* Caldwell 10; *When I hear:* Steinberg 251; *A sound:* Settel 150; *Republicans don't like:* Adler 176; *The Republicans have:* U.S. Congress 125; *The Republican Party:* PP 1948 771.

### POLITICIANS

*I'm proud:* New York *World Telegram and Sun,* April 12, 1958; *A statesman:* New York *World Telegram and Sun,* April 12, 1958; *A great politician:* Ferrell 1980b 306; *There are more:* Ferrell 1980b 282; *The difficulty:* Settel 38; *You can tell:* Hillman 196; *If you don't:* Donovan 29; *I think:* Truman 1973 543; *Many of us:* Truman 1960b 44; *There is:* Truman 1960a 53.

### POLITICS

*Politics is a fascinating:* Hillman 198; *Politics is . . . a game:* Harnsberger 228; *I have always:* Truman 1956 499; *Politics is the ability:* Truman 1989 346; *If you are for it:* PP 1950 179; *Politics—good politics:* PP 1952–3 220.

### POLLS

*I wonder:* Ferrell 1980b 310; *It isn't:* Ferrell 1980b 310; *A man:* Truman 1956 196.

### THE PRESIDENCY

*The presidency is:* Truman 1960b 3; *The presidency will:* Aurthur August 1971; *Being:* Truman 1956 1; *I do not know:* Truman 1956 361; *No president:* Poen 1984 253; *Lincoln:* Gallen 118; *To be president:* Truman 1955 ix; *The greatest part:* PP 1952–3 1197; *Presidents:* Truman 1989 16, Gallen 75; *The United States:* Truman 1989 20; *First:* Settel 136; *You have:* Truman 1960b 82; *It's almost:* Settel 134; *Any man:* Truman 1956 199; *If you don't:* Settel 133; *The president of:* Hersey 69; *He has more:* Ferrell 1980b 239; *A good president:* Truman 1989 79; *I've said:* U.S. Congress 43; *County judge:* Daniels 366; *The president spends:* PP 1949 123; *He is:* Ferrell 1980b 239; *If a president:* Truman 1989 19; *A man with:* Truman 1960a 216; *A president cannot:* Truman 1956 196; *A strong president:* Truman 1989 81–2; *A man in:* Ferrell 1980b 119; *A president may:* PP 1948 819; *The president of:* Harnsberger 247; *Anybody can be:* Robbins 148.

### THE PRESIDENCY OF HARRY TRUMAN

*I've never:* Ferrell 1980b 270; *In the White House:* Truman 1960a 50–1; *Nobody but:* Ferrell 1980b 176; *I am:* Thompson 36–7; *The president:* PP 1948 334; *I think:* Ferrell 1980b 127; *I sign:* PP 1952–3 1198; *I am:* Hillman 232; *It seems:* Smith 57; *There are:* Thomson 141; *Adlai:* McCullough 891; *Some of:* Truman 1960b 9; *I have tried:* PP 1952–3 270.

## THE PRESIDENT'S FAMILY AND ASSOCIATES

*The White House:* Truman 1960a 197; *I have often:* Vernon 46; *I do not know:* Truman 1960a 201; *There is:* Hillman 23–4; *It would be:* Hillman 24; *I'd say:* Truman 1989 99; *It's hell:* Ferrell 1980b 40; *A yes-man:* Truman 1956 416; *I do not like:* Truman 1960a 228–9.

## THE PRESIDENT IN RETIREMENT

*Two hours:* Donovan 16; *I am now:* Settel 129; *I still don't:* Ferrell 1984 239; *You can't:* Ferrell 1994 239; *They are trying:* Truman 1960a 181.

## THE PRESS

*If you have:* Truman 1989 50; Gallen 48; *The objective:* Gallen 51; *Lies:* Ferrell 1980b 194; *If you want:* Truman 1973 258; *Our means:* Truman 1956 414; *The press:* Kirkendall 289; *I've always:* Vernon 19; *You should:* Truman 1960a 31; *No man:* Gallen 50; *It makes:* Williams 183; *When you read:* PP 1948 235; *When the press:* U.S. Congress 168; *I never cared:* Gallen 50; *I have been told:* Williams 20; *Editors:* Hillman 232; *They are always:* McCullough 820; *I find:* Williams 194; *In the picture:* Ferrell 1980b 38; *To hell:* Simpson 1988 370; *I'm saving:* Hersey 43.

## RELIGION

*All the religion:* Steinberg 119; *If men:* PP 1946 142; *Material:* PP 1950 463; *I myself:* Gallen 120; *I'm a Baptist:* Ferrell 1980a 33-4; *Those who:* Truman 1960a 132; *I rather:* Hillman 227; *Who is:* Truman 1973 74; *My Grandfather:* Truman 1960a 128; *Religious stuffed shirts:* Ferrell 1980a 33-4; *I've always:* Ferrell 1980a 33-4; *I've come:* Poen 1982 29.

## ROOTS

*I can remember:* Ferrell 1980a 118; *My home town:* Ferrell 1980b 406; *I've had:* Kirkendall 240; *A man:* Robbins 18.

### THE VICE PRESIDENCY

*A president:* Steinberg 348; *There's an old joke:* Truman 1989 45; *The vice president:* Truman 1989 45; *I bet:* Daniels 232; *Jefferson:* Truman 1989 216–7; *Do you:* Steinberg 209.

### WAR

*Starting a war:* Donovan 81; *I have always:* Truman 1956 383; *The one purpose:* Truman 1956 x; *I was:* PP 1952–3 1200; *Warfare:* Truman 1955 210; *Victorious nations:* PP 1946 187; *We have:* PP 1947 165; *If we do not:* U.S. Congress 126.

### WASHINGTON, D.C.

*Rumors are:* PP 1945 418; *If you want: New York Times,* March 10, 1989; *There are more:* Ferrell 1980b 72; *Woodrow Wilson said:* PP 1948 326; *I have had:* Truman 1960a 89.

## *Harry Truman's Life Stories*

*Precocity:* Steinberg 21; *Dad:* Steinberg 15; *Colonel Crisp:* McCullough 63; *Young Republicans:* PP 1950 296; *Four-Eyes:* Hillman 159; *Childhood Sweetheart:* Robbins 49, Hillman 161; *A Straight Plower:* Kirkendall 351, Steinberg 251, Truman 1973 540, Ferrell 1994 172; *Tending Bar:* Truman 1955 121–2; *Worthy of a Kiss:* Kansas City *Star* July 1, 1976; *Agricultural Science:* PP 1948 550, Kirkendall 126; *Preparing for the Presidency:* Ferrell 1983 201, Daniels 83; *A Late Proposal:* Truman 1973 59, Hillman 192; *Thoroughly Scared:* Hillman 193; Ferrell 1984 50; *The Battle of Who Run:* McCullough 123; *Pedestrian*: Ferrell 1984 50–1; *Philosophy of Business:* McCullough 62; *Politicians and Prostitutes:* Aurthur, August 1971; *A Fate Worse Than Death:* Truman 1960a 156, Ferrell 1980b 271; *Hung Over:* Truman 1973 65, Robbins 62; *How to Do Business:*

McCullough 182; *A Contrary Cuss:* Daniels 147; *One Mad Mom:* Steinberg 97, Truman 1973 73; *The Right Stuff:* Daniels 118, Steinberg 63; *Green Grows the Senator:* Daniels 177, Steinberg 119, 122, McCullough 213; *Housing:* Steinberg 123, 125, Ferrell 1994, 128–9, 413, Smith 55; *Freshman Jitters:* Truman 1955 142, 144; *A Workhorse:* Kirkendall 325, Steinberg 135; *Most Popular Senator: Playboy,* June, 1978; *A Common Man:* Steinberg 135–6; *Best Qualified:* Steinberg 134; *Snot-Nosed:* U.S. Congress 30; *Double-Time:* McCullough 281; *No Hunting:* Steinberg 137, Truman 1960a 84; *No Shame:* Truman 1973 187, Kirkendall 189; *Doing the Right Thing:* Daniels 205; *A Stiff Old Senator:* Ferrell 1980a 74–5, Truman 1973 148, PP 1949 36, PP 1950 110; *The Truman Committee:* Strahan, 1–3, 66–7, 105, 139, 220–2; *Equal Treatment:* Hersey 41; *A Reluctant Candidate:* Truman 1973 167; *On Board:* Ferrell 1980a 90; *Change of Address:* Daniels 255; *Friends:* Steinberg 229; *Just Whistle:* Steinberg 231; *A Fateful Message:* Truman 1955 4–5; *Leftovers for Dinner:* Ferrell 1980b 16; *Morning Prayers:* Truman 1955 19; *Commiseration:* Smith 222–3; *Maternal Wisdom:* Truman 1955 44, Hillman 114, Ferrell 1980b 19; *A House Guest:* Truman 1955 219–20; *Absent-minded:* Thompson 24; *Walking:* Truman 1960a 87, Truman 1973 229–30, Smith 56; *Father-Daughter Communion:* Truman 1973 441; *Souvenirs:* Weddle, unnumbered page; *Tiddlywinks:* Steinberg 249; *Lincoln Slept Here:* West 60–2; *Self-Reliance:* Poen 1984 223, Truman 1981 24, Steinberg 13, 249, Truman 1960a 58; *Making Amends:* Truman 1960a 118–20, Kirkendall 159; *A Real Drink:* Smith 59; *Upstairs on the Front Porch:* Smith 57; *An Overqualified Page-Turner:* Hillman 203, McCullough 427–8; *No Fooling:* McCullough 435; *Top Secret:* Truman 1955 415, Kirkendall 14, Gallu, unnumbered page; *Tough Decision:* Ferrell 1984 146, Ferrell 1994 214, Truman 1973 567, Dayton *Daily News* April 11, 1995; *V-J Day:* Phillips 69; *What Real Gentlemen Prefer:* West 259, Kirkendall 358; *I'll Christen You:* Steinberg 249, McCullough 576; *Sounds Like Him:* Hay 187; *No*

*Manure:* West 78, U.S. Congress 142; *Talk to Bess:* Caldwell 41, Steinberg 291; *Trimming the Guest List:* Ferrell 1980b 67–9, Ferrell 1994 189; *Kicked Around:* Truman 1973 294–5; *Just Call Me Harry:* Steinberg 265; *Old Novocaine:* Acheson 149–50; *Hustling Winnie:* Clifford: 100–104, McCullough 487; *Buzzing the White House:* terHorst and Albertazzie 127–9; *Fertilizing Ohio:* terHorst and Albertazzie, 126–7; *Mother Knows Best:* Steinberg 294, Poen 1984 211, Ferrell 1980b 367; *Thinking of You:* McCullough 623; *The Truman Plan:* Truman 1973 353; *Duplicate Plans:* Daniels 334–5; *Chivalry Lives:* Kirkendall 390, Pemberton 118; *Friend of Israel:* McCullough 607, 620, Steinberg 308; *Reconstruction:* Kirkendall 10, 58, Leuchtenburg, Truman 1973 8, 392, Truman 1956 183; *Giving 'em Hell:* Robert J. Donovan, *Conflict and Crisis: The Presidency of Harry S Truman* 1945–1948 (New York: Norton, 1977), 420, Truman 1956 210, Clifford 226, Thompson 15; *Whistle-Stopping:* Phillips 215, Steinberg 324–5, Truman 1973 23; *Dressed for the Occasion:* McCullough 626; *How to Catch Cold:* Steinberg 325, Ross 87; *Oompah:* Fredericks 18–9; *A Skeptic:* Clifford 234–5; *A Good Night's Sleep:* Truman 1956 220–1, PP 1949 109–10, Robbins 122–3; *An Honest Man:* Allen 6–7; *Crow* en glâce: McCullough 718–9; *RSVP:* McCullough 725; *Insolence:* Clifford 72–3, Acheson 717–8; *Studies in Probability:* Hersey 136, Steinberg 137; *Card Sharp:* Clifford 70; *Lobbying:* Thompson 41; *Tabloid Justice:* Hersey 138; *Friendship:* Pemberton 153–4; *Loyalty:* Hillman 198; *Blowing Smoke:* Goodman 110, McCullough 803; *Outplacement:* Leuchtenburg, Phillips 350; *A Good Host:* Hechler 54; *A Nemesis in Need:* Williams 196; *Lovebirds:* West 111–2; *A Tough Day at the Office:* Kirkendall 13, Acheson 460, Ferrell 1994 328; *Nerves:* Steinberg 337, Truman 1973 441; *The Loss of a Friend:* Truman 1973 499–500; *A Mad Dad:* Thomson 104, Truman 1973 501–3, Williams 187–9, McCullough 827–30; *Something in Common:* Hechler 28; *Second Thoughts:* Ferrell 1984 222; *A Tough Move:* Steinberg 418; *A Disliked Ike:* Truman 1960a 19–20, Truman 1973 557,

McCullough 921-2; *Get a Grip:* McCullough 930, Poen 1984 259; *Unemployed:* Goodman 174; *Lawn Care:* Truman 1960a 86, Truman 1973 664, Hay 276; *Hard Feelings:* Robbins 20; *Where Were You When I Needed You?:* Truman 1960a 57–8, Truman 1964, Truman 1973 567; *No Mooching:* Ferrell 1980b 352; *Big Spender:* Poen 1982 154; *A Striking Resemblance:* Steinberg 420–1, Truman 1960a 62–3; *A Yank at Oxford:* McCullough 956, Ferrell 1994 395-6; *No Hard Feelings:* Ferrell 1994 442; *Sensitivity:* Phillips 433–4; *Empathy:* Truman 1973 567–8; *Still Reading:* McCullough 986; *No Problem:* Poen 1984 269; *Shave and a Haircut:* Aurthur, August 1971; *Priorities:* Aurthur, September 1971; *No Friend Forgotten:* McCullough 985; *Close to Home:* U.S. Congress 117, McCullough 988, Truman 1986 432; *Up in Smoke:* Truman 1981 16.

## *Love, Harry*

Margaret Truman: Truman 1981 24–5.

*4/21/45:* Williams 41; *5/13/45:* Ferrell 1980b 23; *6/12/45:* Ferrell 1984 148, McCullough 398; *7/3/45:* Truman 1955 331, Poen 1984 190, McCullough 404; *7/18/45:* Truman 1973 269; *8/12/45:* Truman 1973 284; *9/22/45:* Ferrell 1980b 69; *12/28/45:* Poen 1982 172–3; *2/25/46:* Ferrell 1980b 86; *6/12/46:* Truman 1981 65; *8/9/46:* Ferrell 1983 529–30; *8/23/46:* Truman 1973 339, Truman 1981 69; *2/19/47:* Ferrell 1980b 109–10; *9/28/47:* Poen 1984 215; *11/14/47:* Truman 1973 356, Ferrell 1980 118–9; *12/3/47:* Truman 1981 102; *6/28/47:* McCullough 580; *8/18/48:* Ferrell 1980b 146–7; *10/5/48:* Ferrell 1980b 149–50; *9/8/49:* Ferrell 1980b 163–4; *10/29/49:* Ferrell 1980b 167; *11/28/49:* McCullough 755; *9/24/50:* Ferrell 1980b 194–5; *11/17/50:* Ferrell 1980b 198–9; *11/22/50:* Ferrell 1980b 199; *12/20/50:* Ferrell 1980b 205; *5/19/51:* Poen 1984 246–7; *6/25/51:* Ferrell 1983 564–5; *1/28/52:*

Ferrell 1980b 234–5; *5/11/52:* Ferrell 1980b 248-9; *2/2/52:* Ferrell 1980b 236–7; *11/25/52:* Poen 1984 257–8; *4/10/55:* Hechler 31; *8/20/55:* Poen 1984 262; *3/19/56:* Truman 1981 123–4; *2/11/58:* Ferrell 1980b 356–7; *9/29/58:* Ferrell 1980b 369–70.



## *Dear Diary*

*4/12/45:* Ferrell 1980b 16; *5/27/45:* Ferrell 1980b 38; *6/1/45:* Hillman 118, Ferrell 1980b 40; *6/5/45:* Ferrell 1980b 42–3; *6/17/45:* Ferrell 1980b 47; *7/7/45:* Hillman 122, Ferrell 1980b 48; *7/25/45:* Ferrell 1980b 55–6; *9/20/47:* Ferrell 1980b 66–7; *Mid-12/47:* Hillman 133–4; *1/6/48:* Ferrell 1980b 122; *2/2/48:* Ferrell 1980b 122; *2/8/48:* Ferrell 1980b 123; *2/14/48:* Ferrell 1980b 124; *7/16/48:* Ferrell 1980b 144; *9/14/48:* Ferrell 1980b 149; *11/1/49:* Hillman 143, Ferrell 1980b 168–9; *6/30/50:* Ferrell 1980b 185; *8/15/50:* Ferrell 1980b 188; *12/9/50:* Hillman 36, Ferrell 1980b 204; *2/20/52:* Ferrell 1980b 238–40; *6/1/52:* Ferrell 1980b 251; *11/20/52:* Ferrell 1980b 274; *5/20/53:* Ferrell 1980b 292; *7/8/53:* Ferrell 1980b 293; *2/2/55:* Ferrell 1980b 313; *6/56:* Ferrell 1980b 336; *1/21/60:* Ferrell 1980b 385.

## *Press Relations*

Truman: Gallen 47

*1/31/46:* PP 1946 102; *2/28/47:* PP 1947 157; *4/3/47:* PP 1947 192; *9/2/48:* PP 1948 460; *12/2/48:* PP 1948 955; *2/10/49:* PP 1949 131; *3/3/49:* PP 1949 157; *4/7/49:* PP 1949 202; *6/16/49:* PP 1949 294; *3/30/50:* PP 1950 234; *4/13/50:* PP 1950 252; *4/17/52:* PP 1952–3 273; *1/15/53:* PP 1952–3 1190–1, 1196.

## *My Fellow Americans*

*6/28/45:* PP 1945 150; *10/3/45:* PP 1945 362, 365; *1/7/48:* PP 1948 13; *6/12/48:* PP 1948 335; *9/18/48:* PP 1948 498; *9/20/48:* PP 1948 518; *9/21/48:* PP 1948 527; *9/23/48,* Merced: PP 1948 549; *9/23/48,* Fresno: PP 1948 550–1, McCullough 661; *10/14/48:* PP 1948 786; *10/26/48:* PP 1948 864; *2/24/49:* PP 1949 145–6; *5/12/50:* PP 1950 377; *10/25/50:* PP 1950 686-7; *12/17/52:* PP 1952–3 1085–6; *1/15/53:* PP 1952–3 1197–1202.

# Index